Make Your Own

ANGEL
BLESSING
SCROLLS

Claire Nahmad has experienced vivid angelic contact since early
childhood. It has been said of her books that they conjure
the actual presence of angels and lift the reader into the angelic
dimension in a way that other books about angels do not achieve.
Claire has published a number of books on healing, herbalism,
magic, folklore and angel lore, and they have a strong following
world-wide, in particular *Angel Healing*.
She lives in North Lincolnshire, England.

By the Same Author

Love Spells
Cat Spells
Garden Spells
Dream Spells
Fairy Spells
Earth Magic
Magical Animals
The Enchanted Garden
The Cat Herbal
The Book of Peace
The Fairy Pack
Summoning Angels
The Secret Teachings of Mary Magdalene (with Margaret Bailey)
Your Guardian Angel
Angel Healing
The Secret of the Ages
Angel Messages

Make Your Own

AПGEL
BLESSIПG
SCRΘLLS

Inspiration for Gifts of
Healing, Hope and Joy

Claire Nahmad

WATKINS PUBLISHING
LONDON

This edition first published in the UK and USA 2010 by
Watkins Publishing, Sixth Floor, Castle House,
75–76 Wells Street, London W1T 3QH

Text Copyright © Claire Nahmad 2010

Claire Nahmad has asserted her right under the Copyright, Designs
and Patents Act 1988 to be identified as the author of this work.

All rights reserved.
No part of this book may be reproduced or utilized in any form or by
any means, electronic or mechanical, without prior permission in writing
from the Publishers.

1 3 5 7 9 10 8 6 4 2

Designed and typeset by Jen Cogliantry

Printed and bound by Imago in China
British Library Cataloguing-in-Publication Data Available

Library of Congress Cataloging-in-Publication Data Available

ISBN: 978-1-906787-94-3

www.watkinspublishing.co.uk

Distributed in the USA and Canada by Sterling Publishing Co., Inc.
387 Park Avenue South, New York, NY 10016-8810

For information about custom editions, special sales, premium
and corporate purchases, please contact Sterling Special Sales
Department at 800-805-5489 or specialsales@sterlingpub.com

CONTENTS

ACKNOWLEDGEMENTS

Thanks are due to the historic peoples of the Western Isles of Scotland for the poetry, beauty and potency of their spirituality, as expressed in their charms, blessings and songs, from which I have drawn fulsomely in creating the blessings for this book. Thanks are also due to Alexander Carmichael, for collecting the blessings before they were lost to our heritage; to Fiona Macleod, for ever being my guiding spirit; to the angel artist Johanna, for introducing me to Azara, Pyrhea and Cathonic via her deeply inspired book, *The Angels of the Rays* (Oughten House Publications); and to Alison Bolus, my editor, for sorting me out.

HOW TO USE THIS BOOK

Part I guides the reader through a step-by-step preparation of a traditional angel blessing scroll – the examples given are: the Blessing Scroll for the Birth of a Child, the Blessing Scroll for Protecting a Child During Pregnancy and Birth and the Blessing Scroll for a Newborn Child – explaining all the different elements that comprise this special form of blessing, such as the Rune of Intent and the Supplication to the Celtic Deities. To assist visualization and attunement, full details are given of all the angels and deities involved with each blessing. These are then followed by suggestions regarding which symbols, crystals and aromatic oils are most relevant to the crafting of each scroll, as well as detailed guidance on recitation and inscription of the blessing, to ensure that it is imbued with angelic potency.

Angel blessings can simply be written on a long piece of paper and rolled up to form a scroll, as was traditionally done, after which they should be secreted in a suitable location. Anyone can make angel blessing scrolls, as artistic ability is not a requirement. However, if you have prepared a blessing scroll that is to be a gift, or if you wish to craft a shorter form of the blessing to display, then you might want to add some suitable decoration. Many suggestions are provided here, from stencilling and stitching to calligraphy and gilding, although you are, of course, welcome to employ whatever artistic skills you have.

Part II of the book provides the full text for a further thirteen blessings scrolls in addition to the three that are reproduced as examples in Part 1, along with with helpful suggestions for suitable symbols and appropriate embellishment.

Finally, a Compendium of Angels provides a valuable reference source regarding the attributes and specific symbols linked to each angel.

INTRODUCTION

This book introduces a beautiful way to marry the act of blessing with the creative healing power of the angels. The result is the release of a gentle but stupendous positive force that works magic in our lives.

Crafting angel blessing scrolls is a simple and original method of drawing on angelic blessings and focusing them with power, stability and intent, while calling on the steadfastness, unfaltering stamina and ever-flowing replenishment of the angels themselves to maintain the current of the blessing being given forth.

The aim of this book is to present a direct and practical method of combining our human gift of blessing with that of the angels. Creating a blessing scroll while consciously attuning to the angels objectifies our intention and helps us to ground and seal the positive affirmation that supplies the framework of our act of blessing. It is similar to setting up an altar and making an offering.

The angel blessing scrolls given in this book are all based on forms of the Celtic blessings, prayers and charms of antiquity, particularly those collected by Alexander Carmichael in the *Carmina Gadelica*. They are simpler to prepare than their original Celtic forerunners, and direct contact with the angelic spheres is sought while producing them. In essence, however, they are a faithful reflection of their original form, and just as magical in their benign and secret outworkings. In addition to these full-length blessings, there are also shortened versions suitable for displaying within the home, though note that each displayed blessing needs to be partnered by a secreted full-length blessing for it to have its power.

Shown here is a shortened blessing worked in the form of a sampler. This makes a delightful way to display the words of a blessing, and the stitched letters, along with any suitable decoration, have a simple charm.

ARDOUSIUS, ARDOUSIUS, ARDOUSIUS,
CALM FLAME OF PUREST BEAUTY,
ARMISAEL OF THE MERCIES,
ENCIRCLE (---) IN YOUR SHINING ARMS
    OF STRENGTH.
POUR UPON HER THE BALM OF YOUR
    FRAGRANT HEART.
HOLD HER IN THE KINDLY FIRE OF
    THE GENTLE ROSE
AND IN THE HALLS OF THE HIGHEST
    ANGELS.
HOLD HER IN THE BRIGHT STAR OF
    GOODNESS,
AND IN THE RAYS OF YOUR
    COMPASSION AND BLESSING.
ENCOMPASS HER IN THE BRIGHTEST
    BLESSING OF HEAVEN,
AND BE THOU TO HER A FORTRESS
    OF SURPASSING LIGHT.
LEND YOUR POWER TO HER BRINGING
    FORTH,
LEND YOUR PROTECTION TO HER
    DELIVERY.

On this shortened version of the
Blessing Scroll for the Birth of a Child, a repeated 'V' symbol
for a bird in flight symbolizes the Celtic deity Epona.

9

The Origin and Meaning of Blessing Scrolls

Blessing scrolls have been a facet of many cultures. They seem to have originated in Ancient Egypt, which may have imported them from an earlier Mesopotamian tradition. However, the first Celts, whose lineage can be traced back directly to Egypt, developed and refined their usage to a degree whereby blessing scrolls became an integral expression of the unique magical and visionary Celtic ethos.

Its shamanic priesthood, the Druids, made wide use of them. Druidic priests and priestesses would create a magical inscription as a blessing for the benefit of a child, a partnership or a friendship; for fertility, both human and agricultural; for some person, animal, site, tree or plant in need of healing or protection; to sow seeds of harmony, happiness and creativity; to turn an enemy into a friend; to attract general good influences; and for numerous other purposes.

The blessing scrolls were concealed in an appropriate place, and their power was renewed from time to time by the Druid presiding over the ritual, who used angelic forces both to create and to reinvigorate the blessing. Essentially, Celtic blessing scrolls were runes (charms) or prayers, inscribed in earliest times on bark and leaves, scraps of wood and animal skin, and on smooth stones. Later, rolls of parchment or paper were used.

The time of inscription relied on certain tides of the moon and the position of the stars. They were essayed at special hours of the day presided over by particular archangels and spirits, and were then secreted, accompanied by a simple ceremony, in a hidden place within the walls or floors of a building, or a niche in a stone, a grove, a garden or a tree.

The idea was that the charmed prayers would be taken into Anwyn (the Celtic otherworld or paradise, pronounced 'Anoon') to provide a connection between the inner and outer worlds.

Benign influences, invoked by the blessing scroll, would then pour through this mystic and hidden gateway, enfolding the place or the persons it was created for in spiritual protection, healing and blessing.

The Importance and Power of Blessing Scrolls

The act of blessing is magical. Human blessing carries great power. It need not (and, we might say, should not) be restricted to formal ceremony. It should rather flow forth freely, without the need for ritualistic paraphernalia. When we consciously ally our human power of blessing to that of the angels, we create a dynamo of transformative, God-sourced energy that can work miracles.

Whilst it is true that there is no actual need for ritual or the tools of ritual, simple ceremonies certainly do help to focus, stabilize and clarify our intent. They create a magnetic point with which the angels connect when we ask them to empower and enrich our offerings of blessing.

The blessing scrolls are a transaction between angels and human beings that offers a way to keep angelic forces grounded, directed and replenished. They comprise a method of filling your world with the wonder of active and almost tangible angelic presence. A few of my own experiences using this method of angelic blessing include:

- ⊕ the healing of a willow tree and a much-loved pine tree
- ⊕ the restoration to health of my entire garden, which had become blighted with an all-encompassing withering disease
- ⊕ a polluted pond that cleared and naturally restocked itself with wildlife
- ⊕ a favourite woodland that was about to fall to industry becoming a protected area
- ⊕ a raucous neighbour who almost overnight became a friend

PART I

HOW TO MAKE ANGEL BLESSING SCROLLS

Blessing scrolls can be basic and unadorned, or they can be works of art. Anyone, whatever their level of artistic ability, can make angel blessing scrolls. What is important is to enjoy the crafting of each blessing scroll, to connect with your material creation at the deepest level of your being as you bring it into manifestation, and to offer your handiwork to the angels on whose power and inspiration you draw in giving forth your act of blessing. In this way, such acts become as a bright mirror, reflecting the secret essence of the angels and transforming our mundane world into a receptacle for miracles.

The principle of blessing is that of self-giving without seeking any return, and this must be the bedrock of all such work. It is essential that in creating a blessing scroll we centre ourselves in the true act of blessing, which is accomplished by sending forth an output of unconditional love. We trust that this love, this blessing, will hit its mark. It is almost as if it is none of our business how and when this happens. Ramifications and timing are entrusted to the wisdom of the divine influences on which we call, which will always ensure the most benign outworking.

PREPARING A WORKSPACE

Simply choose a space where you will feel happy, relaxed and comfortable. It might be outdoors, or in some favourite corner of your home. You need only ensure that it is clean and airy, and that you will not be unduly disturbed during the time that you have set aside to work on your scroll.

It is as well to clear your working space at every level before you begin. The quickest and easiest method is to call on the cleansing angels to perform this task with you. Relax and feel your mind enveloped in quietness. Let your mind sink softly into your heart, and breathe in the stillness that arises from this centre. See the stillness become radiant, and, within the heart of that radiance, put out a call to the cleansing angels to irradiate your working space and purify your aura. Wash your hands in this perfect radiance, which is in its essence the brightness of the angels. The entire process need take only a moment or two. Now you are ready to begin.

ATTUNING TO THE ANGEL

No matter what time of day or night it might be when you start or resume work on your blessing scroll, always take a moment to attune to the angel of the hour and day.

The Angel of the Hour

Various tables exist that list the angels of the hours, but as these tables conflict, it is less confusing just to seek a direct attunement. You will feel the influence of the angel in your work without having to worry about titles, names and designations.

The Angel of the Day

In just the same way, seek the touch and the blessing of the angel of the day. These are known conventionally as:

SUNDAY:	Archangel Michael	*Sun*
MONDAY:	Archangel Gabriel	*Moon*
TUESDAY:	Archangel Khamael	*Mars*
WEDNESDAY:	Archangel Raphael	*Mercury*
THURSDAY:	Archangel Sachiel	*Jupiter*
FRIDAY:	Archangel Haniel	*Venus*
SATURDAY:	Archangel Cassiel	*Saturn*

Do not feel bound to the rigidity of this listing, however. Let a sense of the angel – an inspired communion – be your guide. For instance, the angels above are in masculine mode, and generally belong to an ancient Hebraic interpretation of life. These angels bear many other aspects, other truths, of which perhaps the most important to realize additionally is the feminine expression of their qualities.

The Celts, for instance, would have perceived them very differently from their biblical heritage. The magic and the wild wonder of the Celtic perspective on angels is a wellspring of inspiration, and will be introduced as we progress to angelic attunement as the vital ingredient in the creation of blessing scrolls.

MAKING TWO SCROLLS

If you choose a method of crafting your scroll that is intricate and labour-intensive, you may well wish to keep it and display it. If you are giving away your artwork as a gift, the recipient may feel similarly. As we are translating the blessing scroll craft from ancient Celtic times to contemporary requirements, the good news is that it is possible to retain your blessing scroll. All you need do is make a second scroll to secrete in the required location. Whilst the first may be elaborate, the second can be consummate in its simplicity! As long as it is created alongside the first, and is crafted with the same intention, both your displayed and secreted scrolls will still create a powerful conduit for angelic benefaction.

Your choice of materials and the size of your scroll will be guided by your selection of subject and also by whether you are making a full-length or shortened version. If it is your wish to make an unusually thoughtful and heart-centred gift for a friend or a relative, or if you wish to display your blessing scroll after crafting it, you will probably wish to create two scrolls. Of course, the display scroll, with the abridged blessing, will be shorter than the one made to be hidden away. You may feel that you would like to channel artistic effort into the scroll that is to be hidden, and of course this would bear a special significance in that you would be making a dedicated gift to the otherworld and to the higher sphere of the angels.

As mentioned, for aesthetic and practical purposes the scroll that you intend to display can contain a shortened version of the given blessing. It need not include the Supplication to the Celtic Deities or any other material, although it is important to intone or chant the full blessing and supplication while crafting it in order to give power to your overall act of blessing. Shortened blessings for display purpose are provided at the end of each full-length blessing in Part II.

MATERIALS

You can work in any medium that pleases you. The emphasis for the full-length blessing, though, is on the idea of a scroll – so something that secretes its contents. When rigid materials were used, the ancient Celts wrapped them in leaves or grasses before burying or hiding them, so it is an advantage to bear this in mind. The blessings are often of sufficient length to be a challenge to anyone but the most artistic and dedicated to complete in anything other than writing. This does not mean that they cannot be beautiful, however (although, of course, it is perfectly fine for them to be simple and straightforward and written in handwriting only as good as you can muster!). Some graceful calligraphy, and perhaps an illuminated-style first letter to each verse, can create a striking impression. The essential point to note is that the scroll must not be machine-produced. It has to be crafted with your will and intent, via your hands and heart, or it will remain an empty vessel.

You will need a long (in some cases very long) piece of paper to write the full blessing on. The best solution is to buy some A3 paper (by single sheets or on a pad) and cut each sheet in half lengthways to give you two long strips. If you have a cutting mat, a scalpel and a long metal rule (and a steady hand!) you can do this yourself, but otherwise take it to a craft shop or printers and ask them to guillotine it. You can then tape the two lengths together using invisible adhesive tape (with the tape on the back of the scroll) for a virtually invisible join.

When it comes to the shorter versions of the blessings, made for display purposes, you can indulge your artistic abilities to the full, using many different media and styles, from needlepoint to stencilling, via colourwashes and gilding. You can also add more decoration than would be considered suitable (or practical) for a secreted scroll, which has to be rolled up. Choose from flower petals, crystals, charms and motifs, amongst other things, and make your display scroll a thing of beauty. (It is timely to point out here that the angels are forever constructing beautiful edifices from the realm of symbol and colour, which they free-handedly give to us as gifts of blessing. These living edifices remain for a while in our etheric surroundings, emanating, fostering and directing beautiful forces into our lives.)

Decoration

Beautifying the scroll with decorative features can enhance its evocative potency. Use natural objects such as shells, grasses, hand-made lace, feathers, crystal chippings, leaves, bark, petals, seeds and rosebuds. If you wish to use commercially produced items, it is a good idea to intersperse artificial objects with natural ones. Artificial objects such as miniature silk flowers and seed pearls (even dolls' house items are sometimes appropriate) can create a compelling effect and are readily available from craft shops. Overall, however, blessing scrolls do not lend themselves to glitter and bling! What emanates from them must be in harmony with angelic frequencies, which do not include sentimentality or superficial prettiness. Sweetness and tenderness, however, are qualities that are in tune with the angels.

Blessing Your Materials

Whether your intended blessing scroll is to be simple and basic or a beautiful work of art, it is important to bless your workspace and all the materials you will be using before you begin. I have found that the most effective way to do this is just to hold everything in the white or golden light of the six-pointed star for a moment, while asking aloud for a blessing from the angel of the star who resides at its centre. The star is a point of exalted consciousness – our connection to the Divine – that resides within the heart. We find it by entering the silence within, drawing the breath gently and calmly as if through the heart, and seeing the star shining both at the mid-point of our being and above us in the spiritual skies.

Imbuing the Scroll

If it is your wish, each blessing scroll can be imbued with the influences of aromatic oils, flowers and crystals. How these substances correlate with the angelic kingdom will be explained in the case of each individual scroll.

Whether or not you choose to make use of such properties, it will increase the power of your blessing scroll if you light a candle to help you remain focused and in meditative mode as you work, and if you include the presence of living flowers within your work space. Music, too, is a delightful accompaniment. Music by the master composers, or authentic Celtic music with a spiritual theme, is ideal.

COMMUNING WITH ANGELS

It is a good idea previously to attune to the angel you will be calling on during the actual ceremony of constructing your blessing scroll before deciding on the materials, method and decoration you would like to use. In this way, you will be inspired according to the nature and focus of the blessing you wish to bestow, and the influence of the angel who presides over it.

Now you are ready to start writing your blessing scroll using the wording from the relevant blessings provided in Part II.

BLESSING SCROLL FOR THE BIRTH OF A CHILD

Our first example concerns the offering of a blessing to protect a mother during birth. Before beginning any preparation, you might typically sit quietly to seek angelic attunement concerning your chosen blessing mission.

The Angels

Draw close to Ardousius (Ardoo-shee-us), who presides over childbirth. Begin by softly chanting the name of the angel for a few moments. Let the sound you produce be gentle and soothing, and lead you into a quiet meditative state in which you can read the following words, yet stay centred in your deeper self.

Ardousius brings to our higher senses a wonderfully subtle fragrance of the rose, of the divine feminine spirit. Her heart is like an enchanted cave secreting jewels, or a sacred valley filled with rejoicing flowers. Throughout her being the radiation of inner fires moves as in musical cadences of starry brightness and poignant softness.

Feel her warmth surround you like a kindly embrace. Her eyes are radiant amber pools of nurturing love. Throughout her form sweeps a wave of turquoise blue, which tenderly relieves pain, and a golden swathe of vivid light, which sweeps away fear and danger. Rays of amethyst light and of rose light shine forth with a mystical luminosity from her brow. Her lips move in constant, compassionate blessing. Behind her and around her, the birthing angels dance in perfect formation, creating beautiful geometric forms and adding their power and protection to hers. They are led by Armisael, ministering angel of the womb. Above her stands Brigid, glorious golden one, both angel and goddess, woman of compassion and all-encompassing protection. Adding his light to theirs, Archangel Michael stands as guardian of the spiritual sphere that they inhabit.

The Celtic Deities

You may wish to evoke the Celtic deities. To enhance your blessing power for safe delivery, call on:

- ✠ *Arduinna*
- ✠ *Coventina*
- ✠ *Druantia*
- ✠ *Epona*

Arduinna is a Celtic goddess of the forest and patroness of wild boar. Her name is intriguingly reminiscent of Ardousius, and in fact we see this protective angel of childbirth expressive of her full power in Arduinna. A wonderful feminine expression of mighty strength and courage flows from Arduinna, which is there to serve the woman you wish to bless. Ardousius harmonizes the spate of this torrent by expressing it also as a self-replenishing flow of benevolence. This kindly flow is objectified by the easy and plentiful flow of breast milk that Ardousius fosters, while her twinned self, Arduinna, stands behind her as marshal of her power and holder of the secrets of the sacred

Coventina of the Living Springs,
pure as the swan's breast,
give the healing of your soothing waters
in blessing to this birthing woman.

Briantia, star fire of the forests,
gracious one of the Holy Flame,
give your perfect protection
in radiant blessing to this birthing woman.

Fotla, mistress of Air,
bend your brow in blessing to this birthing woman,
let the might of the powerful she-eagle
sound forth in her cries,
and let her cries deliver her
from pain and travail
that she may bring forth
in safety, ease and joy.

By Brigid, by the great chief of the angels may it be so.

Rose leaves and petals, together with gem chippings,
decorate the edge of this blessing scroll.

forest, which concentrates solar force. Her colours are green and gold, the first denoting the heart and the last the sacred ring of everlasting light, which is the indwelling god force in creation.

Coventina is a goddess of sacred springs and healing wells. She is dressed in white, the perfect radiance of purity. Her magic is of the living waters, the waters of life. She grants safe childbirth and eases the violent force of the delivery. Her essence is kindly and loving, and she works with Ardousius to enable their combined angelic and exalted human influences (a stream from the heart of the goddess) to reach the birthing mother.

Druantia is the fir-tree goddess, protectress of mothers and of infants prior to, during and after birth. She is a deity of fire, and the fir (fire) tree whose essence she expresses is the holder of many mysteries, especially of the pineal gland or the third eye, which looks like a pinecone and opens and closes similarly. She is a coruscating tower of light, and she gives a steadfastness, an unassailable wisdom and a reassurance we can feel from great ancient trees if we attune sensitively to them.

Epona was the horse goddess of the ancient Celts. The white horse with which she is associated is linked to the concept and living presence of the dragon, the sacred serpent. The idea is that the fleet horse is the perfect manifesting vehicle for these wondrous feminine dragon powers to come into full expression on Earth. The horse is the steed for their nobility. The seated woman is the serpent or the fiery soul and spirit essence, the horse beneath her is not only the human body but also its manifold subtle vehicles dwelling within its chakra centres. (The chakras are points on the body aligned with the spine and reaching to the head. They are associated with the ductless glands and are centres of reception for powers and influences flowing to us from the inner worlds, where physical and subtle reality interface and interchange their energies.) We can see how this supremely symbolic goddess is mistress of the forces that generate fertility, birthing and motherhood. Her colours are red, white and black.

Materials and Decoration

Having attuned to the spheres of the angels and the Celtic deities for guidance and inspiration, it is time to decide how to make your scroll. Since a blessing scroll for protecting a mother during birth might be regarded as a private form of the art, you may wish to craft just a single full-length scroll to be hidden away. It is entirely your choice as to whether you decorate it or not. If you do wish to add decoration, you will need to work with a scroll of a reasonable size that can still be rolled and secreted.

You will need a long length of paper to write on (see page 18). You may decide that coloured inks (or indeed ink of a single standard colour) will provide the best medium for the blessing. The words for the scroll are given below, but naturally you can alter or improvise, if you wish.

What might you use to decorate the scroll? Tune in again to the presiding angels and deities. What guidance do they offer?

Perhaps for Ardousius you might select rose leaves and rose petals. (You can varnish these so that they keep their shape and don't wither or split, though they still tend to lose their colour over time. If you object to this, you can add a subtle touch of gold or silver before applying the varnish.) Small pieces or chippings of crystals, or miniature 'jewels' of coloured and faceted glass on sale in craft shops, would indicate the jewels secreted in this angel's heart. A star emanating rays would suggest her fiery, love-centred protection.

For Arduinna, a tiny silver bow or quiver (they can be created from craft materials and then silvered), or a small garland made of minuscule leaves, such as those belonging to the hawthorn tree, might appeal. For Coventina, a single piece of clear quartz could be used to symbolize a drop of water. For Druantia, pine needles or a miniature pinecone might conjure her essence. Epona's symbols are a white horse and a dragon, and also a bird, as she represents the element of air. If you are not artistic, a simply drawn plume of fire, a horseshoe or a 'V' symbol, representing a bird in flight, are suitable images that you could use as substitutes on your scroll.

You might select any or all of these items for the crafting of your scroll. You may decide to use all or several of the colours indicated in the descriptions of the deities and angels as washes for the background of the scroll, as applications of paint or some other medium, or as a range of coloured inks. Your own guidance will inspire you in making the most beautiful and appropriately adorned scroll for the purpose you seek to fulfil. Alternatively, you may wish to work almost entirely upon the inner spheres and use no decoration or colour whatsoever, except for the colour of the ink you use to inscribe the blessing. It is just a matter of deciding how you can best infuse the scroll with your full concentration of power and intent. You may find the art of decoration either distracting or inspiring. Your inner guidance will indicate the correct way for you.

Preparation

At the point where you are ready to begin to create your blessing scroll, you will have:

⊕ *selected your working space and cleared it with angelic help*
⊕ *purified your aura and washed your hands in ethereal light*
⊕ *chosen and assembled your materials and bathed them, yourself and the area in which you work in the pristine light of the six-pointed star*

⊕ *called upon the angel of the day and the angel of the hour to bless your activity*

⊕ *attuned quietly to the presiding angel and deities who will empower your blessing, initially to seek inspiration for the design of the blessing scroll and now, for a second time, to enter into their presence and supplicate their aid in summoning, activating and directing the blessing forces whose focus is the pregnant woman you wish to help (the blessing scroll acts as what might be termed an aiming and charging device)*

Angelic Contact

This is the point where it is vital to enter into deepest communion with the angels, and also, should you wish to include them, with the deities, whose exalted consciousness occupies a similar sphere of elevated purity. Just sit quietly, chant the angelic name given, and begin to feel the essence, the spiritual force, of the being you summon. Work with one entity at a time, and allow yourself the space and duration you need to call them into your sphere of perception.

You are not seeking their personality as such, because many snares lie in wait for our perception when we enter the limitations and the disruptive emotional play of this particular arena. This is because we tend to become embroiled in emotive attachments, and to lose sight of the broader and higher arena, which is the true context of individual personalities.

We need instead to seek the highest spiritual point of which we can conceive, and consciously move away from the restrictions, bondage and pettiness that hold sway on Earth. We can indeed allow ourselves to perceive the individuality, the beautiful uniqueness, of those we supplicate. This is the source of their spiritual potency, their gift from the divine. In a waking dream, W. B. Yeats heard a voice that revealed to him that the love of

God for each member of creation was incalculable, because in each case, no other individual being could satisfy the unique resonance of love found in God's heart. And so we seek the exquisite rendering of this divine uniqueness without descending into the imprisoning aspects of personality, which confine our perception to mundane boundaries through which the winds of the spirit and also the encompassing wisdom of the heart cannot pass.

This bridge between a vast impersonal presence that is so far removed from us that we cannot touch it with our deeper being, and a restricted and stultifying idea of personality that inhibits our access to our deeper being, takes care, skill and an activation of our spiritual will to cross. The trick is to ask our own guardian angel to assist us in the task. Then we will perceive the magnitude of the angels and deities to whom we seek to draw close while simultaneously experiencing the beauty and inspiration of their personal presence.

Begin by entering into the peace and silence that lie within your deeper being, and practise the art of inspired reading, whereby what you read of the angels and spiritual presences is only a starting-point for your own meditations and perception. Let the angels and the spiritual presences quietly enter the sphere of your inner seeing, your soul. Here, they will pulsate with life, with a radiant greeting, and you will know them as friends as well as benevolences. When you have absorbed their presence, you can begin your request for their gift of blessing and protection.

The Blessing

Call on them by intoning the words given overleaf, or use your own, first summoning Ardousius and Armisael, the presiding angels for this particular act of blessing:

'Ardousius, Ardousius, Ardousius,
Calm flame of purest beauty,
Armisael of the mercies,
Encircle (the name of the person to be blessed) in your
shining arms of strength.
Pour upon her the balm of your fragrant heart.
Hold her in the kindly fire of the gentle rose
and in the halls of the highest angels.
Hold her in the bright star of goodness
and in the rays of your compassion and blessing.
Encompass her in the brightest blessing of heaven,
and be thou to her a fortress of surpassing light.
Lend your power to her bringing forth,
Lend your protection to her delivery.'

For every act of blessing, it is strongly recommended that you call on Brigid, the highest and purest of the Celtic goddesses, who appears as a measurelessly radiant woman of lustral fire, giving forth her joy, compassion and love, and the strength and inspiration of her spirit, to all humankind. Brigid overlights the divine feminine in us all, and is a protectress of women in childbirth.

It is also advisable to call concurrently on Archangel Michael. Archangel Michael was known to the ancient Hebrews, and is described in the Bible. However, the forerunners of the Celts honoured him as their supreme masculine guardian long before the birth of Abraham, and his essence has been recognized in Britain in the great protectors Bran, Gweirydd, Arthur and St George (a later rendition of Gweirydd). Archangel Michael is also associated with the symbol of the dragon. Like St George, he is often portrayed as slaying the dragon of the lower self with the sword of truth. This allows the exalted dragon within us to shine forth – the 'pen' or head dragon whose essence protects us.

Recite the Prayer to Brigid and Michael:

'In the name of Brigid the Shining One,
In the name of the Great Chief,
I ask that my prayer for blessing be heard.
I ask that you purify my intention
And make my mind a mountain pool of clarity,
The fish in it leaping and silver
To summon the brightness of the blessing
From the hills of the angels.
May the Archangel Michael, and Brigid the Radiant
In whom dwells the presence of Divine Mother,
Of their benevolence,
Hear and grant my prayer.

By Brigid, by the Great Chief, may it be so.'

The four Celtic deities given for the Blessing Scroll for the Birth of a Child represent the four elements of earth, air, fire and water. If you wish to call on them, you may like to use these words, supplicating each one to add their blessing to that of Ardousius, Brigid and Michael:

'Arduinna, Mighty One,
Give your power of earth,
Of the charge and the victory,
In blessing to this birthing woman.

Coventina of the Living Springs,
Pure as the swan's breast,
Give the healing of your soothing waters
In blessing to this birthing woman.

Druantia, Star Fire of the forests,
Gracious one of the Holy Flame,
Give your perfect protection
In radiant blessing to this birthing woman.

Epona, Mistress of Air,
Bend your brow in blessing to this birthing woman.
Let the might of the powerful she-eagle
Sound forth in her cries,
And let her cries deliver her
From pain and travail
That she may bring forth
In safety, ease and joy.'

Preparing the Scroll

Having summoned and called upon the angels and deities, you are now ready to begin work on your scroll.

If you wish to use crystals, suitable choices would be rose quartz, smithsonite, amber and moonstone, which resonate with the respective angelic spheres of love, consolation, protection and regeneration. You will need to wash the crystals before using them. Simply hold them under a running tap for a second, or pour spring water over them. Hold each one individually to your heart for a moment, asking them to release their healing and blessing powers into the spiritual current you are creating via your blessing scroll. Place them in prominent positions around your working space so that you can connect with them while you work. Set the crystals on your scroll in a circle at its centre for an hour or so after you have finished working on it.

If you want to use aromatic oils, choose lavender, which is connected to the angelic spheres of protection, consolation and peace. Release the fragrance in an oil-burner and breathe it in.

Your first task is to intone the following Rune of Intent (you do not need to write it down):

'As I, (say your name), inscribe this scroll, I affirm that my act is holy, my heart pure, and my words vessels which I pray will be filled and blessed with the power of valiant Michael, Brightness of the Mountains, and Brigid of the Mantle, she who dwells in the golden heart of the sun. May Brigid and Michael bless and protect me and the work that I seek to achieve.'

Now write the words of the Blessing on the scroll, intoning each line slowly and clearly, with powerful intent, before you transcribe it. This is the crucial part of making the scroll. These words are those that pertain to the individual presiding angel concerning the nature of the blessing you wish to project. In this case, they relate to the angel Ardousius.

You can also write the words of the Supplication to the Celtic Deities. If there is not enough space, write a short form, such as:

'Arduinna, Mighty One, add your power of blessing to this work;
Coventina, Merciful One, add your power of blessing to this work;
Druantia, Radiant One, add your power of blessing to this work;
Epona of the Fleet Spirit, add your power of blessing to this work.'

Before doing so, however, it is vital to call once more on the deities and intone the complete supplication for their blessing, even if you inscribe the shortened version on your scroll. This final infusion of intent helps to seal the power of the scroll.

Seal the energy of your blessing scroll by writing the final words of the prayer to Brigid and Michael at the bottom of the page:

'By Brigid and by Michael, Great Chief of the Angels, may it be so.'

When you have finished writing, you can begin work on any decoration you wish to add to the scroll. Throughout, from communion, supplication and inscription until your work is complete, it is important to focus on your purpose, which is to channel the angelic energies and consciousness into the receptacle you are creating to receive the blessing power that you are summoning.

This receptacle is your prayer, your intent, your earnest desire that the person you have named should be helped and, ultimately, the blessing scroll that you are taking such care to create. There is a certain quality that must be infused into the work – a heart-flame, a desire to serve and to bring back spiritual gold from the angelic realms and the exalted worlds of the deities as a selfless gift, a will towards self-giving for the sake of the person you wish to bless. This is the magic that will make your blessing scroll potent.

If you do not complete all the necessary work in a single sitting, it will be necessary to repeat the entire procedure on each occasion that you resume your task, until it is finished. Of course, this does not include rewriting the wording of the scroll.

Each time you finish your work, either to begin again at a future date or because your scroll is complete, thank the angels, and the deities and the crystals if you choose to make use of them.

Once your scroll is finished, roll it with care and tie it with grasses or a length of white ribbon. Seal it by visualizing an equal-sided cross of bright silver in a ring of light encompassing the entire scroll. Dedicate it to the light, to the highest sphere of which you can conceive, by speaking your intention and asking the angels to be present.

Secreting the Scroll
It is now time to secrete your scroll. If you do not wish to part with it, or you are giving it to a friend who may wish to keep it,

ARDOUSIUS, ARDOUSIUS, ARDOUSIUS,
CALM FLAME OF PUREST BEAUTY,
ARMISAEL OF THE MERCIES,
ENCIRCLE (____) IN YOUR
SHINING ARMS OF STRENGTH.
POUR UPON HER THE BALM OF YOUR FRAGRANT HEART
HOLD HER IN THE KINDLY FIRE OF THE GENTLE ROSE
AND IN THE HALLS OF THE HIGHEST ANGELS.
HOLD HER IN THE BRIGHT STAR OF GOODNESS,
AND IN THE RAYS OF YOUR COMPASSION AND BLESSING
ENCOMPASS HER IN THE BRIGHTEST BLESSING OF HEAVEN,
AND BE THOU TO HER A FORTRESS OF SURPASSING LIGHT.
LEND YOUR POWER TO HER BRINGING FORTH,
LEND YOUR PROTECTION TO HER DELIVERY

*Stencilling the words of an angel blessing creates an unusual scroll,
and the stencilled decoration complements the words.*

33

it is important to make a similar unadorned scroll that you can hide away in a special place. In the case of the Blessing Scroll for the Birth of a Child, a niche in a tree or among its roots is best, or perhaps a place around the hearth, if it can be pushed between or under stones without producing a fire risk. If you opt for the roots of a tree, you can bury it in a container (choose one that will do no harm to wildlife). Take care to select the tree with the help of the angels, as in this way the tree itself will add its own safeguarding and benevolence to your act of blessing.

As you secrete the scroll, call on a guardian angel to remain with it and to direct its intent of blessing to the designated mother until such time as its work is done. Give this instruction clearly and definitely.

From time to time (perhaps once a month in the case of this particular scroll, or even once a week, depending on how near delivery the mother is at the time that you finish the scroll) it will be necessary to perform the blessing ceremony of supplication and statement (without, of course, working on an actual scroll). It need only take a few moments, although if you can sometimes light a candle as you intone the prayers, the recharging of your intent by the angels will take a more concentrated form.

As an extension of this act of blessing, which you might have undertaken if there is likely to be a risk to the designated mother, you may choose to make an additional scroll to protect the child throughout its gestation and during birth (see page 35).

If you have decided to make a plain full-length scroll for secretion and a shortened scroll for display, you could be more adventurous artistically, such as in the example on p.34, where the shortened blessing has been stencilled onto the paper (which would be an onerous task for a full-length blessing but is quite a different matter for a shortened one!). In addition, the border has been decorated with angel outlines.

BLESSING SCROLL FOR PROTECTING A CHILD DURING PREGNANCY AND BIRTH

Before beginning, tune in to the presiding blessing angel, and chant the angelic name. As you bring the other angels involved into the field of your inner perception, intone their names too.

The Angel

The angel Afriel is described as an angel of force, of the supreme power of the heavens. There is a likeness to Archangel Michael in that the divine masculine aspect of this angel shines forth with a mighty radiance, casting bright circles of protection outwards from his heart, which encompass and fortify those who call on him.

Yet at his heart, his source, is enshrined the divine feminine essence of Afriel. She manifests as a beautiful black Madonna, bearing a form very much like Isis. At her heart is a six-pointed star, which burns with a coruscating intensity of white-silver light. The star combines the two aspects of the angel in a perfect androgyne. This exquisite being emanates divine force, sweeping its wings in encircling pulses of love, upliftment and protection.

Above Afriel stands Brigid, glorious golden one, both angel and goddess, woman of compassion and all-encompassing protection. Adding his light to theirs, Archangel Michael stands as guardian of the spiritual sphere that they inhabit. Beside them stands Sandalphon, great bright angel of the Earth and angel of the embryo, stretching out arms of incandescent power to protect the child you seek to help and add his blessing to that of Brigid, Michael and Afriel.

There is a tenderness, an almost human kindliness, that streams from Afriel. This angel forbids any hurt, any danger, to approach. Melt into the divine gaze of the angel Afriel and carry the idea of the child you wish to protect, the vibration of its soul, deep into that golden radiant world of which the angel's eyes are a manifestation and a portal.

Feel the Michael force and the Brigid-Isis force (there is a very deep connection between these two) of this mighty angel enfold the child in exquisite wings that shield, protect and encircle in a triumph of God's perfect bright-rayed love.

The Celtic Deities

If you wish to invoke the Celtic deities, attune to them in the same way.

⊕ *Bran*
⊕ *Druantia*
⊕ *Dana*

Bran the Blessed is an ancient British sun deity, to whom the Celts paid tribute for his prophetic skills and his powers of guardianship. His symbol is the raven, considered to be the most intelligent bird species on Earth. He was known as Bran of the Wounded Thighs, and in fact this connects him with the Fisher King, the true Father God, who mourns and bleeds because his beloved consort and source, Divine Mother, has been torn away from him. This marks Bran as one who knows, one who is connected to divine wisdom. He is the all-powerful Father because he understands his oneness with the all-powerful Mother. He has undergone the terrible wounding of the death forces at their most pernicious and has emerged triumphant and whole, filled with the glory of the undiminished sun.

See Bran as a mighty protector, filled with the wisdom of the angels and the ancients. His gaze is one of vast invincible strength. He stands as immoveable as the mountains. There is peace and gentleness in his stance, but he cannot be resisted or thwarted.

Druantia, the fir-tree goddess, presides over holy fire, the living sunlight. She fosters and directs the solar force. She will surround the unborn child from its conception to its birth with an infinitely tender expression and manifestation of this unconscionably powerful energy. See her as an all-loving, nurturing presence, reflecting the gentle might of Divine Mother.

Dana is a Welsh and Breton mother goddess. She is the spirit of Mother Earth, and her creative influences sing and sigh in rivers and streams. She urges all her children to give forth a perfect expression of their life forces. See this vital spirit breathing her life into the foetus and its uterine environment, bringing gifts of protection, stability and timely regulation.

Materials and Decoration

Having communed with the spiritual spheres, you can allow inspiration to flow as to how you will decorate your scroll, should you decide to do so. If it is a scroll destined for secretion, then no decoration is needed, as no one else will see it. If you want to decorate it, however, or if you are making a full-length blessing scroll to give to the mother-to-be, or are making a shortened display version of the scroll, there are some ideas below.

To give a look of antiquity to the scroll, you might like to stain it with a tea wash once all the words have been written on it. Simply leave three teabags in a cup of boiling water to stew for a while, then remove the teabags and brush the solution over the paper using a paintbrush. Not only will it take on the brown colour of the tea, which 'ages' it instantly, but it will also wrinkle slightly with the moisture, so adding to its aged look. Add more coats until you achieve the colour you want. Leave it to dry thoroughly before adding any further decoration.

For images and symbols, you might choose a winged disc and white rose petals (symbolic of Michael) to summon the presence

A friel, Afriel, Afriel,
Tenderly Compassionate One.
Enfold this little soul
In the innermost sanctuary
Which is your heart.

A friel, Afriel, Afriel,
Grand Protector of the helpless,
Shield this child in your bright encircling.
Shield this child from all danger,
From all reversals, from all dismay.

N o harm shall befall this descending soul,
No hurt shall penetrate
The star-bright circuit
Of the victorious Chief of Safeguarding.

S hield downward, upward, roundward,
Shield throughout life, and forever!

Transfer metal leaf adds a touch of glittering light to a scroll.
The winged discs and the pinecones shine out from the paper.

of the male aspects of Afriel. Wheat ears and pearls are associated with Isis, as are the lily and the rose. As a sign of protection, a bright silver equal-armed cross in a ring of golden light can be applied to the scroll.

A ring of angels, signifying Afriel's perfect protection, would be suitable. A piece of clear quartz would provide an emblem of this angel's pure and powerful force of protection.

For Bran, you might select a jewelled ring, the symbol of the intelligence of the raven and the beauty of its consciousness. A leaf or two of sage and a crowned head would be symbolic of this deity, as would a golden pyramid set on its four-square base.

Druantia, in the case of this particular blessing scroll, is best signified by a miniature gilded pinecone.

Dana can be symbolized by a small feather, to signify the holy breath or spirit.

Colours you might select for this scroll include gold, green, fire colours and the soft duns of earth. (If you are inspired differently, it is always best to go with your own flow. An important point, however, is that any blessing scroll involving children should not include black). If the idea of a gilded scroll appeals to you, you might like to apply some shapes cut from sheets of transfer metal leaf around the border (the winged disc mentioned above would be excellent). Transfer metal leaf (an inexpensive form of gold leaf), which comes in little books, is fairly easy to apply, and transforms a scroll into something really special. To apply the metal leaf, simply cut out the shape you want, paint some diluted glue over the area where you want to stick it, then press the metal leaf in place. Smooth out any air bubbles, then peel off the backing paper to leave your gold shape in place. If you are going to put your scroll into a glass-fronted frame, then the metal leaf should be fine, but if it is not going to be protected in this way, apply two coats of varnish (working very carefully).

Suitable crystals would be moss agate, amethyst, rose quartz, clear quartz and amber, which correspond respectively to the angelic spheres of nature forces, harmony, love and protection.

An appropriate aromatic oil would be rose, which corresponds to the angelic spheres of love, joy and purity.

The Blessing

Having assembled your materials and performed the simple rituals of protection and cleansing, you can begin the ceremony of crafting your blessing scroll. Start by entering into communion with the presiding angel once more, this time intoning the Blessing when you are ready.

'Afriel, Afriel, Afriel,
Glorious one,
Defender of the innocent,
Grand protector of the helpless,
Shield this child in your bright encircling.
Shield this child from all danger,
From all reversals, from all dismay.
No harm shall befall this descending soul
Beneath the white splendour
Of your three-cornered shield.
No hurt shall penetrate
The star-bright circuit
Of the victorious chief of safeguarding.
Afriel, Afriel, Afriel,
Tenderly Compassionate one,
Enfold this little soul
In your robes of fragrant light
In the innermost sanctuary
Which is your heart.

Joy of all joys,
Loveliness beyond comparing,
Be thou the cross of glory
To shield downward, upward, roundward,
To shield throughout life, and forever.'

Intone the prayer to Brigid and Michael:

'In the name of Brigid the Shining One,
In the name of the Great Chief,
I ask that my prayer for blessing be heard.
I ask that you purify my intention
And make my mind a mountain pool of clarity,
The fish in it leaping and silver
To summon the brightness of the blessing
From the hills of the angels.

May the Archangel Michael, and Brigid the Radiant
In whom dwells the presence of Divine Mother,
Of their benevolence,
Hear and grant my prayer.

By Brigid, by the Great Chief of the Angels, may it be so.'

Move now, if you wish, to communion with the Celtic deities,
calling on each of them as you gently summon them into your
sphere of vision with this supplication:

'Bran, four-square strong,
Mighty peak of spiritual attainment,
Stand between this child
And all encroaching harm.

Druantia, burst of joyful sunlight,
Flame of the heart of the sun,
Throw forth your rays as a bright halo,
Ringing this child around and around.

Dana, Beloved one,
Heart of the exalted Earth,
Let your Holy Breath
Infuse this child
With the Charm of Righteousness,
With the love of the Great Mother.'

In this particular case, end the supplication with these words, to be pronounced firmly three times:

'The charm of God about thee, little one!
The arm of God above thee!'

Preparing the Scroll

After the pronouncement of this blessing, you can proceed to crafting your scroll, remembering to remain heart-centred and in touch with the angels and the deities as you do so. Gentle, focused breathing will help you to do this As previously instructed, it is important to begin your work of inscription by intoning the Rune of Intent before you begin to write:

'As I, (say your name), inscribe this scroll, I affirm that my act is holy, my heart pure, and my words vessels which I pray will be filled and blessed with the power of valiant Michael, Brightness of the Mountains, and Brigid of the Mantle, she who dwells in the golden heart of the sun. May Brigid and Michael bless and protect me and the work that I seek to achieve.'

Now write the Blessing. If, as in this particular case, the blessing given for any scroll is rather lengthy, there is no need to inscribe it in verse. Instead, you can write it as a piece of prose, which will require far fewer lines.

If you are calling on the deities by writing the supplication you intoned earlier, note that you can, if you prefer, simply write a line for each deity, naming them and asking them to add their power to that of the presiding angel. Don't forget to finish your scroll with the words:

'By Brigid and by Michael, Great Chief of the Angels, may it be so.'

Once you have completed the scroll, thank the angels, deities and crystals, if you chose to make use of them. Leave the crystals in a ring formation on top of the blessing scroll for an hour or two.

Secreting the Scroll

As previously explained, roll and tie the scroll with grasses or a length of white ribbon. Seal it by visualizing an equal-sided cross of bright silver in a ring of light encompassing the entire scroll. Also see the scroll and its blessing intent (you might think of the latter as a pulsating glow of gold emanating from its centre) held securely in a star of light which shines from the heart of the cross. Dedicate it to the light of the Divine, to the highest sphere of which you can conceive, by speaking your intention and asking the angels to be present. You can then secrete it as for the Blessing Scroll for the Birth of a Child (see page 32). However, if you wish to give it to a friend or relative, or if you have used the shortened blessing text (on page 157) because you want to display the scroll, it is important also to make a full-length unadorned scroll that will be concealed.

BLESSING SCROLL FOR A NEWBORN CHILD

Our final example of a blessing scroll is a blessing for a newborn child, given as a benediction on its attributes and life path. It is followed by a checklist of the steps you need to take each time you make a blesing scroll.

The Angels

Archangel Shekinah and Archangel Michael stand as mighty pillars of light to give their blessing and shielding to the child you bring before them. Mikhar and Raphael, presiding angels over the heavenly baptismal waters, wait upon these supreme two, ready to do their bidding in this momentous act of blessing.

Shekinah shines forth with a brilliance that is brighter than all the stars of the universe, yet she does not dazzle or cause human eyes to flinch from her. Instead, she warmly invites you to step onto a silver road that leads straight to her heart. The silver from which this road is composed causes joy to stir and leap in our own hearts. It is called 'the loveliest of all that is lovely', and is the perfect harmonization of gold and silver: the supreme expression of Shekinah and Michael as a single seamless being.

A young woman who bore the Shekinah energies was spoken of as the most beautiful woman ever to have lived. She was known as Mary Hynes, a nineteenth-century Irish girl. Children, women and men fell silent before her, in awe and reverence for her loveliness and the mystical potency of her presence. Her hair, renowned for its enchantment of beauty and the way it seemed to throw off effulgence, was the colour of the path to Shekinah's heart – a wondrous combination of silver and gold.

The pure and radiant soul of Mary Hynes had, with marvellous spiritual skill, blended with Shekinah's essence as a poignant reminder that within each member of humanity lies enshrined the potential to rise even higher than the greatest angels. We can draw inspiration from Mary Hynes and take the road direct to Shekinah's heart in all confidence that we, too, can enter the temple of her heart and become consummate with the limitless love, healing, protection and benevolence that enfold us there.

Within the heart of Shekinah we can stand in the innermost presence of this supreme one, and also enter into communion with Archangel Michael, magnificently radiant. Archangel Michael was the original slayer of the dragon (St George is a human expression of his energies), and his awe-inspiring authority sweeps away every shadow and encroachment. The dragon he felled was the dragon of the lower expression of life – all that corrupts, distorts and darkens perception. Michael himself is often portrayed as a serpent: the golden serpent of supernal consciousness, expressing God. His sacred task is to prevent the lower earthly saurian from swallowing us in its coils and causing us to forget our divine serpent essence.

Shekinah and Michael nurture all that is noble in the human soul. Their arms are filled with an abundance of blessings and gifts for every newborn child who is brought into their presence. Bathe in this ineffable presence. See the child you wish to bless being received into it. The grand and sweet encirclement of Shekinah and Michael will catch you up into bliss.

The Celtic Deities
✥ *Brigid*
✥ *Taliesin*

Brigid was the supreme goddess of the Celts. She was universally beloved, the Druids in particular regarding her as a being of unsurpassed purity and light. She is associated with Shekinah in that this angelic being is an expression of Brigid's own angelic qualities, for Brigid encompasses all worlds. She was called the 'foster mother' of Christ, and indeed she was, because she fostered Christ consciousness in the West long, long before it arrived from the East in truncated form as a religion. She has three aspects: Brigid of the Radiant Flame (her spirit), Brigid of the Divine Forges – the Smithwoman who forges creation from the Radiant Flame (her soul) – and Brigid the Crone, the Ancient of Days, whose mysterious being enshrines the wisdom of the earth and the manifesting physical world of matter (her body). She was known to her people as the Woman of Compassion, the Woman of Healing, the Woman of Inspiration, the Woman of Miracles. Essentially she is the Bride, the feminine aspect of the great Christ being in the heavens, the Daughter of God. Her capacity for blessings and precious gifts of the soul can only be described as bounteous.

Taliesin, Radiant Brow, was said to be the magical son of Cerridwen, a potent goddess whose enchanted cauldron was the source of her vast power. She had taken on a servant, Gwion, an ugly, misshapen youth of stunted growth who served her well. He was instructed to attend her wondrous Cauldron of Inspiration, but never to taste of its contents.

One day, Gwion scalded his finger by accident in the contents of the cauldron, and sucked it to ease the pain. He was instantly transformed into a magician. Cerridwen, on returning, challenged him for his disobedience and set off in pursuit of him. A shape-shifting contest ensued, which Cerridwen won by changing herself into a black hen and eating Gwion after he had taken the form of a grain of wheat.

Nine months later, Cerridwen gave birth to beautiful Taliesin, Radiant Brow, prophet, philosopher, spiritual teacher and peerless bard, who was drawn like Moses from the water in a little rustic vessel. (These special circumstances of his discovery as an infant identify Taliesin, in common with several gods before him, as a deity.) He appeared on earth in human form shortly after the fall of Arthur, and his mysterious poetry, with its cadences of beauty, lives on today. Taliesin came forth from the Goddess as the perfect son of light, transformed by his journey through the underworld of her challenges and transfigured by his final sacrifice. Every gift was given to him, and he in turn will offer every gift and blessing to souls new born into the challenges of their own light.

Materials and Decoration

Seed pearls are symbolic of newborns, as are hand-made lace, rosebuds and acorns. Pieces of eggshell, washed in pastel colours, also signify a birth. Mother-of-pearl provides beautiful, significant decoration for a new life, even if you can find only buttons! A pair of tiny shoes, sprayed with silver, show that the soul is silver-shod, ready to reflect the light of heaven on each step of its journey. Silver and golden coins are emblematic of abundance, as are cornucopias filled with fruit and flowers.

For the angels, their protection is signified by these symbols:
- ⊕ *Shekinah:* an ascending golden bird
- ⊕ *Michael:* white rose petals and a golden, crowned serpent
- ⊕ *Raphael:* a caduceus (two opposing serpents twining around a staff)
- ⊕ *Mikhar:* a dove and a mountain spring

For the Celtic deities, their signs are:
- ⊕ *Brigid:* pearls, dandelion petals, rowan and hawthorn berries, and the sacred spiral
- ⊕ *Taliesin:* the Celtic harp, a star in a pool, a leaping salmon, the symbol of a boat, the symbol of a swan, and swansdown

Colours for this scroll should be delicate pastel shades – nothing dark, heavy or vivid is suitable.

Suitable crystals are clear quartz and rose quartz, which correlate to the angelic spheres of purity and protection, and love, joy and wisdom.

An appropriate aromatic oil is rose, which corresponds to the angelic spheres of love, joy and purity.

The Blessing

Having assembled your materials and performed the simple rituals of protection and cleansing, you can begin the ceremony of crafting your blessing scroll. In this case, the blessing is a little different. Call on the four angels Shekinah, Michael, Mikhar and Raphael, and the deities Brigid and Taliesin, to be present and to focus their blessings on the child while it is given the ancient baptismal blessing in spiritual waters. Hold the child clearly in your thoughts as you do this. Chant the names of the angels and deities, and supplicate their presence by name. Note that this angel blessing is lengthy, so the scroll will need to be a bit longer than normal.

Imagining that these six bright ones stand in a circle around you and the child, facilitating the baptismal blessing, intone these words:

'I bathe thy palms
In showers of wine,
In the lustral fire,
In the seven elements,
In the juice of the rasps,
In the milk of honey,
And I place the nine pure choice graces
In thy fair fond face.

A wavelet for thy form,
A wavelet for thy voice,
A wavelet for thy sweet speech,
A wavelet for thy luck,
A wavelet for thy good,
A wavelet for thy health,

A wavelet for thy throat,
A wavelet for thy pluck,
A wavelet for thy graciousness;
Nine waves for thy graciousness.

Grace of form,
Grace of fortune,
Grace of voice,
Grace of the Son of Peace be ever thine,
Grace of the image of God be thine.

Grace of men,
Grace of women,
Grace of lover,
Grace of sons and daughters be thine.

Grace of eating,
Grace of drinking,
Grace of music,
Grace of guidance,
Grace of sea and land be thine.

Grace of rest,
Grace of journeying,
Grace of silence,
Grace of dreaming be thine.

Grace of the wild duck,
Grace of the swan of the fountain,
Grace of every kindliness and comfort;
Enduring grace by day and by night be thine.

Grace of the love of the skies be thine,
Grace of the love of the stars be thine,
Grace of the love of the moon be thine,
Grace of the love of the sun be thine,
Grace of the love of the crown of heaven be thine.

Thou art the joy of all joyous things,
Thou art the light of the beam of the sun.

The lovely likeness of God
Is in thy pure face,
The loveliest likeness
That was upon earth.'

Recite the prayer to Brigid and Michael:

'In the name of Brigid the Shining One,
In the name of the Great Chief,
I ask that my prayer for blessing be heard.

I ask that you purify my intention
And make my mind a mountain pool of clarity,
The fish in it leaping and silver
To summon the brightness of the blessing
From the hills of the angels.

May the Archangel Michael, and Brigid the Radiant
In whom dwells the presence of Divine Mother,
Of their benevolence,
Hear and grant my prayer.

By Brigid, by the Great Chief of the Angels, may it be so.'

Now intone the Supplication to the Celtic Deities:

'Brigid of the graces,
Brigid of whole-souled loveliness,
Give to this child
The nine pure choice graces.

Taliesin, Radiant Brow,
Encircle this child
With your ring of bright gifts.
Be to this child
The surpassing star of guidance.'

Now intone the Rune of Intent:

'As I, (say your name), inscribe this scroll, I affirm that my act is
holy, my heart pure, and my words vessels which I pray will be
filled and blessed with the power of valiant Michael, Brightness
of the Mountains, and Brigid of the Mantle, she who dwells in
the golden heart of the sun. May Brigid and Michael bless and
protect me and the work that I seek to achieve.'

Now that you have intoned the Blessing, the prayer to Brigid and
Michael, the Supplication to the Celtic Deities and the Rune of
Intent, you can proceed to the inscription of the Blessing, followed

I bathe thy palms
In the lustral fires,
In the seven elements,
In the milk of honey,
And *I* place the nine pure choice graces
In thy fair fond face.

*G*race of form,
Grace of fortune,
Grace of voice,
Grace of the son of Peace be ever thine.
Grace of the image of God be thine.
Grace of men,
Grace of women,
Grace of lover,
Grace of sons and daughters be thine.

*T*hou art the joy of all joyous things.
Thou art the light of the beam of the sun.

*The white-on-blue combination gives this scroll a fresh,
contemporary look, and the coins add a subtle sparkle.*

by the inscription of the Supplication to the Celtic Deities, if such is your choice, and finish with '*By Brigid and by Michael, the Great Chief of the Angels, may it be so*', which should be written at the bottom of the page.

Preparing the Scroll

Here we have written the blessing in bleach on a pale blue background, which gives a striking effect. First paint the paper in a pastel colour of your choice, then, when it is dry, dilute some household bleach with water in a 3:1 dilution. Using a fine acrylic paintbrush, carefully paint the letters on to the scroll. (You might want to practise to gain some proficiency first!) Be very careful not to splash or drip the bleach on to the paper or anything else, including your clothes. When you have finished the lettering, add your chosen decorations before framing the scroll and hanging it on a wall. We have used the image of a dove, again painted in bleach, which looks very effective against the blue 'sky' of the background. Seed pearls decorate the border and silver coins mark each corner. The effect is eye-catching in its simplicity. After any decoration of the scroll, place on it any crystals you may have been using, in the form of a ring, and leave them undisturbed for an hour or so.

Secreting the Scroll

If you wish to make another scroll for display purposes, follow the method above so that the scroll is imbued with all the blessing power of the recited prayers and visualization that you have channelled into the original, and use the words of the shortened blessing on page 167. Use any of the symbols mentioned above, interpreting and including them as you wish. The original scroll should then be rolled up and hidden. This marks the end of the ritual, whether or not you are making a display scroll.

CHECKLIST FOR MAKING A BLESSING SCROLL

⊕ *Select your workspace.*

⊕ *Clear and bless your workspace.*

⊕ *Attune to the angel of the hour.*

⊕ *Attune to the angel of the day.*

⊕ *Seek communion with the presiding blessing angel and the deities.*

⊕ *Having sought their inspiration, decide on your materials for making and decorating the scroll.*

⊕ *Assemble your materials (this might take a few days; when you return to work on your scroll, you will need to repeat the first four steps described above; however, they are brief procedures).*

⊕ *Bless your materials.*

⊕ *Seek communion once again with the angels and deities.*

⊕ *Intone the Blessing.*

⊕ *Recite the Prayer to Brigid and Michael for protection.*

⊕ *Make the Supplication to the Celtic Deities.*

⊕ *Intone the Rune of Intent ('As I, (say your name), inscribe this scroll...' etc.).*

⊕ *Write the Blessing and the Supplication to the Celtic Deities (using a shortened version, if wished), intoning each line before you write it down; remain in communion with the angels and deities throughout.*

⊕ *If you use a shortened version of the Supplication to the Celtic Deities to inscribe on your scroll, or if you dispense with such inscriptions altogether but still wish to evoke the power of the deities, it will be necessary to call on them beforehand and intone the full supplication in each case, even though you will not be writing down the full supplication.*

⊕ *Finish your scroll by writing the words: 'By Brigid and Michael, the Great Chief of the Angels, may it be so.' at the bottom.*

✠ *Decorate your scroll if you wish, remaining in communion with the angels and deities throughout. Alternatively, make a second, shortened, scroll for display, and decorate it accordingly.*

✠ *Once it is complete, place the crystals (if you decide to use them) in a ring on the scroll for an hour or two.*

✠ *Thank the angels and the deities, and the crystals if you choose to make use of them.*

✠ *Roll the completed scroll and tie it with grasses or white ribbon.*

✠ *Seal it by visualizing an equal-sided cross of bright silver in a ring of light encompassing the entire scroll.*

✠ *Dedicate it to the light, to the highest sphere of which you can conceive, by speaking your intention and asking the angels to be present.*

✠ *If you do not wish to part with it, or you are giving it to a friend who may wish to keep it, make a similar unadorned scroll that you can conceal in a special place.*

✠ *Select your hiding place with the help of the angels.*

✠ *Secrete the scroll. (This can be in a niche in the home or outside.)*

✠ *As you secrete the scroll, call on a guardian angel to stay with it and to direct its intent of blessing to its designated destination until such time as its work is done. Give this instruction clearly.*

✠ *Once a month, or perhaps less often (but keep this recharging rhythmical), you should perform just the blessing ceremony of supplication and statement (without working on a scroll).*

✠ *See this stream of recharging power going out to the angel that stands guard over the scroll, who will infuse it with renewed force and maintain the correct direction of its blessing flow.*

✠ *This process of renewal need take only a few moments, although if you can sometimes light a candle as you intone the blessing prayers, the consequent recharging of your intent by the angels will take a more concentrated form.*

(See pages 14–53 for detailed instructions on each step.)

PART II

THE
ANGEL BLESSING
SCROLLS

I
BLESSING SCROLL
FOR PROTECTION FROM NIGHT FEARS,
NIGHTMARES & PSYCHIC ATTACK

Although these forms of sleep disturbance can be dramatic in their expression, the mundane experience of a troubled night's rest on a regular basis can mean that something intrusive at the astral level of life is encroaching on us. This blessing scroll may be used to supplicate relief for these milder problems as well as their more traumatic manifestations.

The Angels

The circle of angels to call upon to protect from malice and attack consists of Shekinah, Michael, Metatron, Nuriel, Rampel and Derdekea.

Shekinah, star-bright archangel of grace and rarefied fire with eyes of radiant love, holds the person to be shielded in her auric warmth of nurturing reassurance. This great archangel walks in the light of the highest heavens.

Michael, brightest warrior and the embodiment of honour perfected, stands beside Shekinah. Great Chief of the angelic realms, he is ready to serve and to attend to every mortal's prayer for protection. His all-encompassing shield is golden, yet casts off albescence, the 'white light as pure as the swan of the wave'. For this particular blessing, we also call on Michael's mystery name, Sabbathiel. It reminds our deeper being that Michael is completion, fulfilment, the closing of the circle. There is no chink in his armour.

Metatron is an aspect of the might of Michael and Shekinah. He is the heavenly scribe, and as such will carry a particular power of blessing and empowerment to the making of your scroll. He is spoken of as the tallest angel in heaven, the Prince of the Divine Presence. He has a peculiar power of vision in that his beautiful, penetrating gaze seems to issue from every part of him, as if he had multitudinous eyes.

It is this stern, yet loving, intensity and ubiquitousness of gaze that dispenses Metatron's gargantuan force of protection in all directions. It casts the light of his fiery countenance into every dark corner, through every misty shroud of disguise.

Nuriel, 'white peace', crowns the unrest of the elements with his command of stillness, so that they fall into calm submission. Any attack or encroachment will use the dynamics of the elements both within and without our minds and bodies. Nuriel, who glows with the soft blues and greens of sky and sea, masters and transforms any elemental charge of hostility. He soothes, tames and commands the raging beast that dwells in the potential of elemental expression.

Rampel radiates wisdom, steadfastness, ancientness, strength and masterful stillness. He gives stability, endurance and inner mastery. See him as an angel within a great mountain – vast, rooted, mighty, centred in stillness. All attacks, when they encounter Rampel, become as little puffs of vapour melted by the sun, with which his heart directly communes.

Derdekea reaches almost beyond the glory of an angel. She expresses angelic consciousness, but she is more than an angel. She shines in Shekinah, and yet manifests in her own right. She is present in Brigid, and might be said to be Brigid's vital connection to God the Mother. She is a heavenly female power who descends to Earth for the salvation of humanity. The Gnostics referred to her as the Supreme Mother. She was known as a teardrop – a drop of the divine essence, descending from God's innermost heart. She is also known as the Holy Grail – the Woman who is All.

The Celtic Deities
⊕ *Fionn*
⊕ *Bran*
⊕ *Morgan Le Fay*

Fionn Mac Cumhail (pronounced Finn mak Kool) was a hero, champion and chieftain. He led the Fianna, a tribe of honourable warriors whose strength, endurance and magical feats were legendary.

Fionn was spoken of as markedly generous, a protector of the people and an upholder of justice and mercy – the true kingly and queenly virtues. The Fianna were famous for their commitment to truth and their defence of the weak and the innocent.

An old Irish poem proclaims, 'We of the Fianna never told a lie. Falsehood was never attributed to us. But by truth and the strength of our hands, we came safe out of every combat.' The Fianna attributed their integrity in battle directly to the integrity of their truth-keeping, and their good fortune to their willingness to give free-handedly to those in need. This pure-hearted chieftain and his noble warriors protect against attack and ward off evil.

Bran the Blessed is an ancient British sun deity, to whom the Celts paid tribute for his prophetic skills and his powers of guardianship. His symbol is the raven, considered to be the most intelligent bird species on Earth. See Bran as a mighty protector, filled with the wisdom of the angels and the ancients. His gaze is one of vast invincible strength. He stands as immovable as the mountains. He holds the power of benign overlooking. There is peace and gentleness in his stance, but he cannot be resisted or thwarted.

Morgan Le Fay is perhaps the most misunderstood of the Celtic deities. She is properly identified as Derdekea, the Divine Drop, so exalted in her humanity that her being encompasses both human and angelic consciousness. Our understanding of Morgan has been purposely (and quite hideously) distorted by forces adversarial to the light and therefore to the progress and general good of humanity. Morgan's affinity, Mary Magdalene, was similarly denigrated.

Morgan's story was revealed by spiritual sources thus: at the end of the fifth century, Tamar, the daughter of Jesus and Mary Magdalene, reincarnated with Joseph of Arimathea as Morgan and Arthur. Arthur married Morgan, his half-sister, making her his queen.

Monks connected with Rome came to his court from Alexandria, purporting to preach the true path of Christ. In fact, they were priests of darkness whose aim was to work through the earthly Church to distort human perception of this sacred 'Way'. They persuaded King Arthur that to have married his half-sister (who was in fact his true soul partner) was to have sinned deeply against Christ, and that, if he did not have the marriage annulled and banish Morgan from his presence, they would both burn in hell forever.

Feeling that he had unforgivably betrayed his beloved Morgan's honour, and that because of his behaviour she might be consigned to hellfire, King Arthur immediately obeyed his priests.

To seal their triumph, the monks arranged for him to marry Guinevere soon afterwards, who was presented to him as his 'solar' bride, 'given' to him by 'Christ' as a reward of solace for saving both his own and Morgan's soul.

This marriage was a fatal mistake, which led to the destruction of Camelot, the city of 'curved light', whose sacred ring would otherwise have saved the world and lifted it into ascension so that the many horrendous conflicts since that time, culminating in the terrible 'years of fire' of the two World Wars, would never have occurred.

Because of Morgan's blessed and holy presence, the era of Camelot was one of the most beautiful to have occurred on Earth. The veil between the worlds of the soul and the spirit, and the world of men, diminished almost to vanishing point, and quests were undertaken in a reality of full consciousness of the soul worlds that could only be undertaken symbolically, with ever-dimming sight and hampered perception, once Camelot had fallen. This truth lies at the heart of the knights' mystical adventures in a realm that is Earth, but a magical Earth.

Morgan is truly the essence of the Holy Grail, the Holy Drop of the divine spirit we call God, and to call on her for protection is to invoke a blessing of the highest order.

Decoration Ideas

Whether you want to decorate a shortened scroll for display purposes or a full-length scroll for secretion, here are some ideas to inspire you.

There are many symbols to denote protection. Some of the most powerful include:

✠ *an equal-sided bright silver cross in a ring of light*
✠ *the Tau (a cross shaped like a T)*
✠ *the crux decussata, or St Andrew's cross (a white X set in a blue circle)*
✠ *the Egyptian ankh, which is shaped like a T topped by an oval like a head*
✠ *a talismanic eye*

For the angels, their protection is signified by these symbols:

✠ *Michael:* a golden, crowned serpent
✠ *Brigid:* some red thread or rowan berries
✠ *Shekinah:* a phoenix
✠ *Nuriel:* a crown of white feathers
✠ *Rampel:* a mountain
✠ *Derdekea:* a teardrop reflecting a star

For the Celtic deities, their signs are:

✠ *Fionn:* a bright blade reflecting the shape of a heart
✠ *Bran:* a golden pyramid
✠ *Morgan:* a jewelled cup

A suitable crystal would be clear quartz, dedicated to the angels of protection, which will connect with the angelic spheres of safeguarding. Clear quartz is supremely receptive to programming and can be used to personalize protection.

An appropriate aromatic oil would be rosemary, which connects to the spheres of protection and shielding. Rosemary is known anciently as the maternal herb, and emanates the shielding mother-force. If it took root naturally outside a home, it was said to be the sign of a dominant female influence.

Writing the Blessing

Before starting work on your blessing scroll, you will have assembled and blessed your materials, prayed to Brigid and Michael and intoned the Supplication to the Celtic Deities. Now intone the Rune of Intent:

'As I, (say your name), inscribe this scroll, I affirm that my act is holy, my heart pure, and my words vessels which I pray will be filled and blessed with the power of valiant Michael, Brightness of the Mountains, and Brigid of the Mantle, she who dwells in the golden heart of the sun. May Brigid and Michael bless and protect me and the work that I seek to achieve.'

Then write the Blessing:

'In the name of Brigid the Shining One,
In the name of the Great Chief,
I pray that (insert the name of the person to be protected)'s soul
Be encircled this night
By the bright circle of angels
Whose holy names
Shall now be made manifest:
Nuriel, Sabbathiel, Rampel,
Metatron, Shekinah, Derdekea,
And the beloved Guardian Angel,
Encircle (-----) round

With silver rings of brightness;
With silver rings of purest brightness.
May the Archangels Michael and Brigid
And the bright circle of angels
Encircle (----)'s soul this night
With silver rings of brightness.

And morn and eve, day and night,
Be the rood of the Nine Angels over (----) down,
From the crown of (----)'s head to the soles of (----)'s feet,
From the crown of (----)'s head to the soles of (----)'s feet.'

(Note that in addition to the Blessing, you will also write the Supplication to the Celtic Deities and a one-line prayer to Brigid and Michael, both below in italic type.)

Intone the Prayer to Brigid and Michael:

'In the name of Brigid the Shining One,
In the name of the Great Chief,
I ask that my prayer for blessing be heard.
I ask that you purify my intention
And make my mind a mountain pool of clarity,
The fish in it leaping and silver
To summon the brightness of the blessing
From the hills of the angels.

May the Archangel Michael, and Brigid the Radiant
In whom dwells the presence of Divine Mother,
Of their benevolence,
Hear and grant my prayer.
By Brigid, by the Great Chief of the Angels, may it be so.'

Write the Supplication to the Celtic Deities:

'Fionn, Prince of the Fianna,
Of the bright encircling blades,
Be with (----) this night and always.

Bran of immensity,
Of the noble brow and the valiant spirit,
Of the mind alight with stars,
Of the soul of the snow-crowned heights,
Add your generous portion
To (----)'s safekeeping
Tonight and forever.

Morgan of mercies,
Of the merciful Secret,
Rose of the Rood,
Fruit of the promised Branch of Glory,
O heart of lustral fire!
Shield (----) from all attack and encroachment,
Each and every night and day.'

Finish the scroll by writing the words:

'By Brigid and by Michael, Great Chief of the Angels, may it be so.'

Now you can decorate the scroll as you wish, before secreting the full-length scroll and displaying a shortened version of the scroll (if made) using the wording opposite.

SHORTEΠED BLESSIΠG FOR THE DISPLAY SCROLL

'In the name of Brigid the Shining One,
In the name of the Great Chief,
I pray that (insert the name of the person to be protected)'s soul
Be encircled this night
By the bright circle of angels
Whose holy names
Shall now be made manifest:
Nuriel, Sabbathiel, Rampel,
Metatron, Shekinah, Derdekea,
And the beloved Guardian Angel,
Encircle (-----) round
With silver rings of brightness;
With silver rings of purest brightness.'

2

BLESSING SCROLL
FOR PROTECTION BY A
GUARDIAN ANGEL

This is a simple blessing scroll that you might make for your own protection, or for that of a loved one. To create this scroll, you will need to make vivid contact with your own guardian angel. If you intend to make the scroll for someone else, it is important to initiate communion with your own guardian angel as well as theirs.

The Angels

Your guardian angel is linked to your zodiacal angel, so when you think of this being of limitless light, think also of the zodiacal angel: Aries (Malahidael); Taurus (Tual); Gemini (Ambriel); Cancer (Muriel); Leo (Verchiel); Virgo (Hamaliel); Libra (Zuriel); Sagittarius (Adnachiel); Scorpio (Barbiel); Capricorn (Hamael); Aquarius (Cambiel); Pisces (Barchiel)

Be aware of its cosmic presence, knowing its lustrous inspiration flows to you through the conduit of your guardian angel.

The great archangel who has all guardian angels in her/his care is Sandalphon, the gentle yet mighty angel of the Earth. Ask Sandalphon to bless your contact with these angels.

When calling on your guardian angel, request to be given its name, or simply say softly 'my guardian angel' as a supplication for its presence. You may become aware of colours, of gentle pulses like wing beats, of a palpable presence in the air around you, which is an exudation and a loving enfolding, as in heavenly arms, of infinite love, safety and a deep, radiant calm.

Continue to develop your relationship with your guardian angel by summoning it, talking to it, and requesting its help on a daily basis. Your life will become greatly enriched by doing so.

Once we get to know our own guardian angel, we can ask it to link to other guardian angels, and indeed to any other angel or sphere we need to contact. This is one of the great functions of the guardian angel. So, if you are making this scroll for someone else, first draw close to your own guardian angel, and then to that of the other person. The two guardian angels will forge a vital link.

The Celtic Deities

⊕ *Brigid*
⊕ *Bran*
⊕ *Morgan Le Fay*

Brigid, beautiful Fosterer of Infinite Light, who is the divine bride and the divine daughter, will stand guard as you call down the blessings for this scroll, emanating the supreme radiance of Goddess (see pages 45–46).

Bran, embracing the infinitude that the mountain peaks touch, will overarch all, becoming one with Sandalphon (see page 61).

Morgan, the Ineffable One, will envelop your soul and its circuit in the rising dew of the bliss of heaven. None can penetrate the shielding of these supernal realms (see page 61).

Decoration Ideas

Whether you want to decorate a shortened scroll to display or a full-length scroll for secretion, here are some ideas to inspire you.

The scroll could be decorated with a pair of white angel wings, as these denote enfoldment, protection and ascension. Your guardian angel can be denoted specifically by a shield. Ornament the shield according to your experience of your guardian angel.

You might like to use the colours that you perceive within the aura of your guardian angel; however, the predominant theme for this scroll should ideally consist of white and gold.

For the angels, their protection is signified by these symbols:

- ⊕ *Sandalphon:* a garland and an orb
- ⊕ *Zodiacal angel:* imagery pertaining to your sign combined with anything that expresses the emanations you feel from this majestic angel

For the Celtic deities, their signs are:

- ⊕ *Brigid:* an equal-sided cross of light within a ring of light (an important seal for this particular scroll)
- ⊕ *Bran:* a white raven
- ⊕ *Morgan:* a jewelled cup with golden snake rising from its bowl

Lavender flowers might be added to this scroll's decoration, or even a little aromatic bag filled with dried lavender.

A suitable crystal would be clear quartz, dedicated to the angels of protection, linked to the angelic spheres of safeguarding.

An appropriate aromatic oil would be rosemary, which connects to the spheres of protection and shielding.

Writing the Blessing

Before starting work on your blessing scroll, you will have assembled and blessed your materials, prayed to Brigid and Michael and intoned the Supplication to the Celtic Deities. Now intone the Rune of Intent:

'As I, (say your name), inscribe this scroll, I affirm that my act is holy, my heart pure, and my words vessels which I pray will be filled and blessed with the power of valiant Michael, Brightness of the Mountains, and Brigid of the Mantle, she who dwells in the golden heart of the sun. May Brigid and Michael bless and protect me and the work that I seek to achieve.'

Then write the Blessing:

'O Guardian Angel of my right hand,
Be you with me this night.
Be you a bright flame before me,
Be you a guiding star above me,
Be you a smooth path below me,
And be a kindly shepherd behind me,
Today, tonight and forever.
Encompass me in your blessing and protection,
O kindly angel of my right hand,
My ever-present Guardian Angel

And stay you, angels,
Stay with me,
The beauteous three
Who are Michael, Brigid and
Sandalphon, bright Lord of Prayer.'

(Note that in addition to the Blessing, you will also write the Supplication to the Celtic Deities and a one-line prayer to Brigid and Michael, both below in italic type.)

Intone the Prayer to Brigid and Michael:

'In the name of Brigid the Shining One,
In the name of the Great Chief,
I ask that my prayer for blessing be heard.
I ask that you purify my intention
And make my mind a mountain pool of clarity,
The fish in it leaping and silver
To summon the brightness of the blessing
From the hills of the angels.
May the Archangel Michael, and Brigid the Radiant
In whom dwells the presence of Divine Mother,
Of their benevolence,
Hear and grant my prayer.
By Brigid, by the Great Chief of the Angels, may it be so.'

Write the Supplication to the Celtic Deities:

'Brigid of Blessings
Abide with me.
Bran the Blessed
Watch over me.'

Morgan of the sublime brow,
Morgan of the secret name,
Weave your holy incantations
Around my soul-shrine
All around my soul-shrine
This night and every night.'

Finish the scroll by writing the words:

'By Brigid and by Michael, Great Chief of the Angels, may it be so.'

Now you can decorate the scroll as you wish, before secreting the full-length scroll and displaying a shortened version of the scroll (if made) using the wording below.

SHORTENED BLESSING FOR THE DISPLAY SCROLL

'O Guardian Angel of my right hand,
Be you with me this night.
Be you a bright flame before me,
Be you a guiding star above me,
Be you a smooth path below me,
And be a kindly shepherd behind me,
Today, tonight, and forever.
Encompass me in your blessing and protection,
O kindly angel of my right hand,
My ever-present Guardian Angel.'

3

BLESSING SCROLL
FOR PROTECTION
ON A JOURNEY

The angels who safeguard our journeys are Michael, Zazriel and Cosmiel. If the journey is to be undertaken on water, the angel Elemiah should also be summoned, and the angelic name added to the inscription of the blessing. Elemiah is the guardian of voyages and maritime expeditions, and appears on the mystical Tree of Life as one of the eight mighty seraphim.

The Angels

Michael, High Chieftain with Shekinah over all angels, stands as a huge sun disc, throwing off great swathes of brightest illumination in rhythmic pulses that encircle the world from horizon to horizon. His blessing is bestowed on those who seek protection and shines as a guiding light before and all around them. Know that the journeyer goes forward in this light.

Zazriel is an angelic prince of the divine strength, might and power. He strides alongside the journeyer, exuding a godly dynamic that causes all that is hostile to wellbeing to fall back and hide its face in abjection.

Cosmiel is an angel so magnificent in her freedom that her unfettered voyagings circumnavigate the cosmos. A whirlwind of spiced and perfumed breezes moves through her, giving exhilaration and the daring spirit of adventure to the journeyer. As she inspires this intrepid and invincible stance, so she simultaneously enfolds the journeyer in wings as bright and powerfully protective as a wayfarer's moon.

The Celtic Deities

⊕ *The Dagda*
⊕ *Donn*

A deity of lifecycles and the seasons, the Dagda is the supreme Celtic Father God. He is the keeper of a magic cauldron out of which everything emerges from a secret source. This mysterious deity presides over outer and inner voyages. He is spoken of thus in a spring paean by the Celtic bards:

'Give praise to the Dagda, Father of All, Lord of Boundless Knowledge, giver of life and of death; in the depths of his sacred halls he makes music on his magic harp, strange and lovely as the

voices of faery birds, which flies to the heart of the deep-breasted Earth, there to call forth into being the round of the seasons; so that forever do they dance back and forth from the stars.'

The Dagda may be called on to add his blessing and protection of the journeyer to that of the angels.

Donn is the Irish and Welsh God of the Wayside and Travellers. In Donn's safe and healing haven the dead were believed to rest on their way to the grandeur of the afterlife. Within the nurturing atmosphere of Donn's house, journeyers could rest and reflectively weave their earthly experiences into knowledge and nourishment for their souls. Donn is a kind friend and protector of travellers, and blesses them all.

Decoration Ideas

Whether you want to decorate a shortened scroll for display purposes or a full-length scroll for secretion, here are some ideas to inspire you.

Charms to bless travellers include an image of a boat, an anchor, a bell, dried beans (which can be silvered or gilded), a frog (a magical beast that can live on earth and in water), the Agnus Dei, images of St Christopher and the St George Cross. A magical cup, like the Grail, is a blessing charm for travellers on water.

The Agnus Dei is a sacred emblem, originating from the earliest civilizations. It is connected to ram, the highest system of mystical knowledge ever to be given to humanity. It depicts a lamb with its head turned, looking out down its spine. From the centre of its spine arise a flag and a cross (the Templar flag, which bears a red cross on a white background, is a powerful symbol to choose in portraying the flag).

St Christopher is represented as a giant man with a beard who is carrying the Christ child on his back over a rushing river.

The St George Cross is similar to a Greek cross. It is emblazoned in crimson on a blue background.

If you are sympathetic to the Christian world view, or if you would like to use the blessings of these saints anyway, add a supplication to them on your blessing scroll.

For the angels, their protection is signified by these symbols:

⊕ *Michael:* a sun disc with wings
⊕ *Zazriel:* huge footprints
⊕ *Cosmiel:* enfolding wings, and a bright star with a boat crossing its face

For the Celtic deities, their signs are:

⊕ *The Dagda:* a harp rising from a cauldron
⊕ *Donn:* a house with smoke rising from the chimney, candles alight in the windows and an open door with a road leading to its doorstep (signifying the House of Solace, of which Donn is host and master)

Suitable crystals would be cerussite and yellow jasper, which respectively attune to the angelic spheres of consolation, vitality and protection, and serenity, integrity and nurturing; black onyx, attuning to the angelic spheres of stability and guardianship.

An appropriate aromatic oil would be rosemary, which connects to the spheres of protection and shielding. The angelic safeguarding associated with rosemary is feminine in nature.

Writing the Blessing

Before starting work on your blessing scroll, you will have assembled and blessed your materials; prayed to Brigid and Michael and intoned the Supplication to the Celtic Deities. Now intone the Rune of Intent:

'As I, (say your name), inscribe this scroll, I affirm that my act is holy, my heart pure, and my words vessels which I pray will be filled and blessed with the power of valiant Michael, Brightness of the Mountains, and Brigid of the Mantle, she who dwells in the golden heart of the sun. May Brigid and Michael bless and protect me and the work that I seek to achieve.'

Then write the Blessing, substituting appropriate wording if the scroll is for you, and adding Elemiah if the journey involves crossing water:

'Bright angels be with you in every pass,
Cosmiel, Michael, Zazriel.
Bright angels be with you on every hill,
Cosmiel, Michael, Zazriel.

Spirit be with you across each stream,
Headland and crest and grassy plain.
Cosmiel, Michael, Zazriel.

Each sea lane and land lane,
Each lane of the pathless air,
Bright angels be at your side.
Cosmiel, Michael, Zazriel,
Be above, below and all around.
Each lying down, each getting up,
In the trough of the waves,
On the ridge of the breakers,
Each step of the journey you are going,
Each measure of the journey you are going,
Bright angels accompany your every breath,
Cosmiel, Michael, Zazriel.

God of All before me,
God of All behind me,
God above me, God below me,
I on the path of God,
God on my track, too.

Who is there on the dry land?
Who is there on the bogland?
Who is there on the wave-strand?
Who is there in the boundless air?
Who is there by the door-jamb?
God of All.'

(Note that in addition to the Blessing, you will also write the Supplication to the Celtic Deities and a one-line prayer to Brigid and Michael, both below in italic type.)

Intone the Prayer to Brigid and Michael:

'In the name of Brigid the Shining One,
In the name of the Great Chief,
I ask that my prayer for blessing be heard.
I ask that you purify my intention
And make my mind a mountain pool of clarity,
The fish in it leaping and silver
To summon the brightness of the blessing
From the hills of the angels.

May the Archangel Michael, and Brigid the Radiant
In whom dwells the presence of Divine Mother,
Of their benevolence,
Hear and grant my prayer.
By Brigid, by the Great Chief of the Angels, may it be so.'

Write the Supplication to the Celtic Deities:

'Dagda of all strength,
Dagda of the wondrous paths of heaven,
Keep me in my wholeness,
Keep me in my peace,
Keep me in all my ways.

In the name of the Dagda,
Father of All,
May this be so.

Donn of the open door,
Donn of sheltering,
Donn of the kindly welcome,
Bless my outward journey,
And bless my homecoming
With the pure blessings of heaven.'

Finish the scroll by writing the words:

'By Brigid and by Michael, Great Chief of the Angels, may it be so.'

Now you can decorate the scroll as you wish, before secreting the full-length scroll and displaying a shortened version of the scroll (if made) using the wording opposite.

SHORTENED BLESSING FOR THE DISPLAY SCROLL

'Bright angels be with you in every pass,
Cosmiel, Michael, Zazriel.
Bright angels be with you on every hill,
Cosmiel, Michael, Zazriel.

Through each sea lane and land lane,
Through each lane of the pathless air,
Bright angels be at your side.

Cosmiel, Michael, Zazriel,
Be above, below, and all around.
Each lying down, each getting up,
In the trough of the waves,
On the ridge of the breakers,
Each step of the journey you are going,
Each measure of the journey you are going,
Bright angels accompany your every breath,
Cosmiel, Michael, Zazriel.'

4

BLESSING SCROLL
FOR PASSING AN EXAM

This blessing scroll will help to give you poise, confidence and swift access to your memory banks as you take your exam. It will attract positive, helpful influences to your performance, and will hone your guesswork to its highest intuitive potential. It can also be adapted to bless the giving of an important presentation or undergoing a job interview.

The Angels

The first of the angels of achievement, Angel Harahel, shines above your head like a star, on hovering wings of benevolence. She imparts a flow of inspiration that calls forth intellectual achievement and flashes of brilliance in the mind. She lights the dim halls of memory in a clear and magnifying light. She silences internal chatter and focuses the concentration so that it is one-pointed and unwavering. She is dramatically silver-bright.

Angel Ambriel is an enfolding, bridging angel whose theme is integration, and yet who manifests the twinned, mirror aspects of our deeper soul reality. She gives the gift of clear communication so that we may relay our understanding without obstruction or hindrance. She brings forth truth from the fermenting mists of confusion. Her colour is a sweetly beautiful mother-of-pearl, which glimmers and glances with an exquisite mystical lustre.

Anthriel is a beautiful angel of harmony and balance. To draw close to Anthriel is to enter into a radiant calm. She restores our poise and our centredness. She transforms our shrill anxiety into the deep resonance of steadfast self-assurance. Experiencing her presence imparts the feeling of being lulled into clarity by the soft whispering of a summer sea.

Barakiel is an expansive, humorous angel who helps us swiftly to retrieve our sense of perspective. Our horizons widen and our perceptual limitations recede when Barakiel draws near. He grants success and good fortune, and allows us to be generous to ourselves.

Cambiel is a beautiful angel who exudes a certain eccentricity: he will sometimes greet you from unexpected angles, almost as if to startle you, and he loves to make you laugh with astonishment! He bestows increased intelligence and the inspired courage to soar beyond 'the box' into heights of unconventional thinking, which comprise the spheres of genius.

Ecanus is the angelic scribe. He shows us how to allow and direct the flow of golden and many-coloured communion with the heavenly realms through the heart intelligence and into our tongue, pen or fingertips, depending on our own particular mode of word-creation. He teaches us that the act of expression at its outermost or physical point, whether it be through the sung, spoken or written word, or through gesture and movement, is a component of this mystical flow, and should properly be conducted as an art in itself – as a balletic and sacred response to it and facilitator of it.

This applies even when we are just using our hands to create words. There are important chakras that extend from the spine down into the centre of the palms, which should make our fingers aware of the flow of consciousness from the heart. Sometimes they can even seem to tingle or vibrate. Ecanus manifests as these flowing streams of energy and consciousness, as if he wears great robes of the clearest streams of water, which are as pure as mountain rills and reflecting every light and colour of the heavenly worlds.

Iahel, the lovely angel of meditation and illumination, bestows the grace of her radiance in a shedding of starry light that flashes with points of coruscating illumination. These intense jewel-points of light catch up our human intuition in their fiery dance, energizing and releasing its potential.

Raphael, with his scintillating aspect Enwo, presides over all, granting his benevolence in an outrush of majestic light. Lord of the Book of Truth, Giver of Laws and Master of the Word of Maa Kheru, this great prince of healing overarches the mystical and the earthly sciences and facilitates the Spirit of Wisdom. He reveals to us that the laws within science and inspired knowledge are indeed healing, holistic forces. Once we learn to use them with wisdom, they will transform us and our world.

The Celtic Deities
⊕ *Gwydion*
⊕ *Taliesin*

Gwydion is a Welsh master magician deity, presiding over bards, music and the arts. Folklore calls him God's Druid. He is associated with crackling sparkles and colourful fiery explosions of inspiration and ingenuity, and is something of a Merlinesque figure! We call on him to help us out of a mental tight spot.

Taliesin, Radiant Brow, peerless bard and magical son of the goddess Cerridwen with her Cauldron of Inspiration, will help us to attain the heights of personal achievement. He teaches that he carries the Cauldron within us. Taliesin knows how to battle against the odds to win his spurs (see page 46).

Decoration Ideas
Whether you want to decorate a shortened scroll for display purposes or a full-length scroll for secretion, here are some ideas to inspire you.

Charms for this scroll include the image of a deer, a scarab (the image of a beetle), a black cat, a crescent moon with a star in its horns, and the sacred sign of the spiral. The Sign of Benediction is associated with luck bringing, and comprises a hand with the third and fourth fingers and the thumb closed, the first and second fingers being outstretched.

For the angels, their protection is signified by these symbols:
⊕ *Harahel:* a silver bird
⊕ *Ambriel:* a silver arched bridge surmounted by a
   golden spiral
⊕ *Anthriel:* a depiction of the number 8 in silver-violet
⊕ *Barakiel:* a smiling winged face

- ✛ *Cambiel:* a hand pointing upwards
- ✛ *Ecanus:* an upright pen portrayed as a maypole with rainbow-coloured streamers
- ✛ *Iahel:* scattered jewels
- ✛ *Raphael:* a miniature golden scroll
- ✛ *Enwo:* a shining finger leaving trails of light as it writes

For the Celtic deities, their signs are:
- ✛ *Gwydion:* a Druid's wand
- ✛ *Taliesin*: a single golden eye

A suitable crystal would be a gold tiger's eye, which is linked to the angelic spheres of stability, pure reason and clarity. You can gaze into this crystal and feel connected to these spheres.

An appropriate aromatic oil would be rosemary, which connects to the angelic spheres of protection and clarity.

Writing the Blessing

Before starting work on your blessing scroll, you will have assembled and blessed your materials, prayed to Brigid and Michael and intoned the Supplication to the Celtic Deities. Now intone the Rune of Intent:

'As I, (say your name), inscribe this scroll, I affirm that my act is holy, my heart pure, and my words vessels which I pray will be filled and blessed with the power of valiant Michael, Brightness of the Mountains, and Brigid of the Mantle, she who dwells in the golden heart of the sun. May Brigid and Michael bless and protect me and the work that I seek to achieve.'

Then write the Blessing, substituting appropriate wording if the scroll is not for you:

'Angel Harahel, star-bright,
Angel Ambriel, beautiful bridge of truth,
Anthriel of the heavenly harmonies,
Barakiel of benevolence,
Cambiel of the dancing lights,
Ecanus of the words of light,
Iahel, illustrious lamp of the sacred inner halls,
Breathe your blessings through and through me.
Shine in me,
And bestow your gifts and inspiration
At my time of testing.

Raphael of the glories,
Of the highest heights of heaven,
And Enwo, your brother,
Give me quicksilver wings of head and feet,
Grant me your golden memory and blessed pen
At my time of testing.'

(Note that in addition to the Blessing, you will also write the Supplication to the Celtic Deities and a one-line prayer to Brigid and Michael, both below in italic type.)

Intone the Prayer to Brigid and Michael:

'In the name of Brigid the Shining One,
In the name of the Great Chief,
I ask that my prayer for blessing be heard.
I ask that you purify my intention
And make my mind a mountain pool of clarity,
The fish in it leaping and silver
To summon the brightness of the blessing

From the hills of the angels.
May the Archangel Michael, and Brigid the Radiant
In whom dwells the presence of Divine Mother,
Of their benevolence,
Hear and grant my prayer.
By Brigid, by the Great Chief of the Angels, may it be so.'

Write the Supplication to the Celtic Deities:

'Gwydion, king of enchanters,
Open the treasure-store within me,
The knowledge deep as tree-roots
That contains and preserves
In a clarity pure as amber
All I have ever learned.

Taliesin, Radiant Brow,
Peerless one of the sunbeams,
Vouchsafe to me
The love of the Bright Ones,
The grace and the good charm of the Bright Ones,
And your own golden benediction.'

Finish the scroll by writing the words:

'By Brigid and by Michael, Great Chief of the Angels, may it be so.'

Now you can decorate the scroll as you wish, before secreting the full-length scroll and displaying a shortened version of the scroll (if made) using the wording opposite.

SHORTENED BLESSING FOR THE DISPLAY SCROLL

'Angel Harahel, star-bright,
Angel Ambriel, beautiful bridge of truth,
Anthriel of the heavenly harmonies,
Barakiel of benevolence,
Cambiel of the dancing lights,
Ecanus of the words of light,
Iahel, illustrious lamp of the sacred inner halls,
Breathe your blessings through and through me.
Shine in me,
And bestow your gifts and inspiration
At my time of testing.

Raphael of the glories,
Of the highest heights of heaven,
And Enwo, your brother,
Give me quicksilver wings of head and feet,
Grant me your golden memory and blessed pen
At my time of testing.'

5
BLESSING SCROLL
FOR PASSING
A DRIVING TEST

This blessing scroll can be used to supplicate blessings for any test that involves physical activity. Ribkiel, the mighty angel of the chariot, drives the power of the blessing. He delights in mediating the life forces that flow between the physical world and the human mind and soul. He bestows outstanding achievement on those who submit to his wisdom

The Angels

Ribkiel is a mighty angel who drives the divine chariot. He is set over the order of angelic life, which manifests as wheels. He rules the driving force in our lives. We can call on him to address the mundane aspects of driving we encounter, but he will also teach us how to be true pilots, steering all the many aspects of the craft that is our life on the path to the summit. Feel the immensity of this dynamic angel. Breathe in his recharging influences. He inspires us to muster our strengths, to mobilize our will, to express our intention. All the cobwebs of lethargy, hesitation and negative resistance fly from us when we commune with Ribkiel. We feel the wind in our hair, at our back, under our feet. We feel ready for take-off – all the components within us that must work together to produce and sustain the necessary energy for our volition, full of vigour, vibrant and raring to go!

Ask this angel's blessing on your forthcoming test, supplicating him to hone your skills, judgment and concentration. He will centre you in your inner seat of power and command.

We also petition Archangel Michael, of the invincible shields and whirling blades of pure intent, to oversee our performance in a driving test. Archangel Michael gives steadfastness and calms nerves. He will inspire confidence and offer protection.

The Celtic Deity
⊕ Taranis

Taranis is the thunder god of Gaul. His symbol, like that of Ribkiel, is a wheel. The Romans eventually adopted him as a deity, associating him with the chariots that they used in warfare. We need to be careful to call on Taranis with respect and wisdom, and in fact we must not do so at all unless we elect the angels to act as mediums.

Decoration Ideas

Whether you want to decorate a shortened scroll for display purposes or a full-length scroll for secretion, here are some ideas.

The Trumpet of Victory, one of the Eight Glorious Emblems of Buddha, is an auspicious symbol for this blessing scroll (the little gold and silver varieties that can be bought as Christmas-tree decorations are eminently suitable). Another of the Eight Glorious Emblems is the vase, which can be drawn as an image. Yet another is the Wheel of the Law. Place an image of the sun at its centre to represent the hub and the spokes. An open hand bearing a jewel is also an appropriate symbol for this scroll, as are three sprigs of white heather.

For the angels, their protection is signified by these symbols:
- *Ribkiel:* the medieval depiction of the sun, which is a face emanating rays in the form of a wheel
- *Michael:* a three-cornered shield of light bearing the image of a golden serpent

For the Celtic deity, his sign is:
- *Taranis:* a drum decorated with the sun shown as a wheel

A suitable crystal would be a gold tiger's eye, which is linked to the angelic spheres of stability, pure reason and clarity.

An appropriate aromatic oil would be rosemary, which connects to the angelic spheres of protection and clarity.

Writing the Blessing

Before starting work on your blessing scroll, you will have assembled and blessed your materials, prayed to Brigid and Michael and intoned the Supplication to the Celtic Deities. Now intone the Rune of Intent:

'As I, (say your name), inscribe this scroll, I affirm that my act is holy, my heart pure, and my words vessels which I pray will be filled and blessed with the power of valiant Michael, Brightness of the Mountains, and Brigid of the Mantle, she who dwells in the golden heart of the sun. May Brigid and Michael bless and protect me and the work that I seek to achieve.'

Then write the Blessing, adapting the wording accordingly if the scroll is not for you:

'Ribkiel of the Divine Chariot,
Ribkiel of might,
Ribkiel following God of the moon,
God of the sun,
God Who ordained to us
The Daughter-Son of Mercy;
Ribkiel who climbs the heights in glory,
Of your grace,
Bless thou my enterprise
So I am brimful of thy strength and surety.

Michael of the shields and the pure bright blades,
Be you between my two shoulders,
Above me and encircling me,
At my time of testing;
And be the Perfect Spirit upon me pouring,
Oh, the Perfect Spirit upon me pouring!
And I the Cup of Grace.'

(Note that in addition to the Blessing, you will also write the Supplication to the Celtic Deities and a one-line prayer to Brigid and Michael, both overleaf in italic type.)

Intone the Prayer to Brigid and Michael:

'In the name of Brigid the Shining One,
In the name of the Great Chief,
I ask that my prayer for blessing be heard.
I ask that you purify my intention
And make my mind a mountain pool of clarity,
The fish in it leaping and silver
To summon the brightness of the blessing
From the hills of the angels.

May the Archangel Michael, and Brigid the Radiant
In whom dwells the presence of Divine Mother,
Of their benevolence,
Hear and grant my prayer.
By Brigid, by the Great Chief of the Angels, may it be so.'

Write the Supplication to the Celtic Deities:

'*I am calling the angels of heaven,*
The angels of the height;
In the name of the Three
I am calling.
Grant me the blessing of Taranis,
The steady eye, the sure hand,
The strength of inspiration.
May I be granted the blessing of Taranis
Through the angels.
I behold mansions, I behold shores,
I behold angels floating,
I behold the shapely rounded column
Coming landwards in friendship to us.'

Finish the scroll by writing the words:

'By Brigid and by Michael, Great Chief of the Angels, may it be so.'

Now you can decorate the scroll as you wish, before secreting the full-length scroll and displaying a shortened version of the scroll (if made) using the wording below.

SHORTENED BLESSING FOR THE DISPLAY SCROLL

'Ribkiel of the Divine Chariot,
Ribkiel of might,
Ribkiel following God of the moon,
* God of the sun,*
God Who ordained to us
The Daughter-Son of Mercy;
Ribkiel who climbs the heights in glory,
Of your grace,
Bless thou my enterprise
So I am brimful of thy strength and surety.

Michael of the shields and the pure bright blades,
Be you between my two shoulders,
Above me and encircling me,
At my time of testing;
And be the Perfect Spirit upon me pouring,
Oh, the Perfect Spirit upon me pouring!
And I the Cup of Grace.'

6

BLESSING SCROLL
FOR A
BUSINESS ENTERPRISE

This scroll can be used at the inception of a business project or to help a struggling business survive during difficult economic times. Each business, however small, has its own designated angel. The business angel inspires directional flow, good practice, and bright ideas. It safeguards, blesses prosperity, and highlights the principle of service.

The Angels

It is important to appreciate that the angels who preside over commerce are no less angelic than others of their kind! Their gifts and inspiration can be imprisoned and dragged to a lower level by human materialism, but this impulse derives from our unenlightened consciousness, never from the angels themselves.

Bearing this truth in mind, it is as well to resolve from the outset always to honour the angelic code of practice in calling on the angels of commerce. The angels always serve the collective good and the highest good. They balance and perfect the outcome of this code by ensuring that individuals are never sacrificed for the sake of the collective good, but that their needs are cared for within the general scheme, so that a happy solution for all is produced. In this way, the needs of the one and the many are brought into harmony and do not betray one another.

Be careful not to use these angelic powers for purely personal or selfish gain. You might think of your business (or that envisioned by or belonging to the recipient or object of the scroll) as giving a worthwhile service and benefiting others as well as yourself. If you keep these ideals and aspirations in mind, you can be confident that you will not be waylaid by emanations from the lower mind!

As well as the angels described below, each business has its own angel. If you would like to discover its name, simply enter into communion with your guardian angel (see p.69), and ask to be connected to your business angel. You can then request to be given its name, which will be helpful in your dealings with it. If the scroll is not for yourself, explain this process to the recipient.

The angels of commerce are Azara, who helps to balance the right brain with the linear-thinking left brain; Anauel, who presides over commercial success and prosperity and protects businesses; Butator, who presides over clarity and precision concerning calculation; Tual, who presides over Taurus and helps us to realize our aims in the material world; Barakiel, who brings an abundance of good things and favourable circumstances; Pyrhea, who gives fire to our creative drive, and Cathonic, who connects and grounds us in our endeavours.

Azara comes to us on the orange ray of creation and helps us to keep a clear head and a balanced, logical power of analysis, even when situations are chaotic and threatening. Call on her to bless your endeavour and sense her beautiful orange life energy.

Anauel throws about him a beautiful light of electric blue, like a tropical fish. This colour ray is good for businesses. Feel his kindliness and the richness of his blessing. He assures you that if you give wisely and generously, you will always receive.

Butator works with Azara to help you calculate on all levels with precision and clarity. He has a good understanding of detail.

Tual gives the bullish strength, determination and capacity for hard work needed to initiate and sustain a business. Tual also shows us how to keep ourselves grounded and refreshed through Mother Earth so that we avoid exhaustion and burn-out.

Expansive Barakiel has a jovial, warm aura, which is a delight to experience. Bathe in it and enjoy his benevolence and cheer.

Pyrhea manifests on the inner planes in a beautiful red light like the glow in the heart of the purest ruby. We might say of her that a little of her power goes a long way! Use her forces cautiously and respectfully. She will give you the fire, the drive, the enthusiasm and vision to get your project underway.

Cathonic works with Pyrhea to manifest and sustain your aspirations at the outer level. She is the light in the heart of jet.

Never use Pyrhea or Cathonic for purely selfish gain.

The Celtic Deities
⊕ *Brigid*
⊕ *Bran*
⊕ *Epona*

The people of the Western Isles of Scotland hailed Brigid as the deity who kept their kitchens stocked with good things. Brigid's bounty and benevolence can be called upon to bless business enterprises rooted in the good of the community.

Bran the protector stands mighty as a monolith, turning back ill tides from our prosperity. This wise warrior encourages us to express high aspirations and live our ideals.

Epona, the horse goddess of the Celts who manifests as a white mare, will bring abundance and fertility to a business project.

Decoration Ideas

Whether you want to decorate a shortened scroll for display purposes or a full-length scroll for secretion, here are some ideas.

You may want to keep the scroll austerely simple by selecting one symbol for prosperity, such as a gilded coin, the eye at the summit of a triangle, or the cornucopia, and to complete the enhancement through colours alone. Alternatively, you may want to overload it with symbols for good luck and prosperity!

It is always a good idea to incorporate the colours electric blue, red, gold and orange into your scroll, and perhaps to include an angel to show that the developing potential of your enterprise is under the protection and guidance of the angels. Tune in to the angel and see it as an image of your guardian angel.

For the angels, their protection is signified by these symbols:
- *Azara:* a tree with invisible roots penetrating into the earth
- *Anauel:* a shower of golden coins
- *Butator:* a magnifying glass, a number 10
- *Tual:* a ring through flaring nostrils surrounded by a halo
- *Barakiel:* a smiling winged face
- *Pyrhea:* a ruby
- *Cathonic:* a pillar

For the Celtic deities, their signs are:
- ⊕ *Brigid:* a dandelion, milk foaming in a pail, and pearls
- ⊕ *Bran:* a monolith carved with a cross
- ⊕ *Epona:* a horseshoe

Suitable crystals would be carnelian, citrine, bloodstone, orange calcite and obsidian, which link to the angelic spheres of abundance, construction and inspired sustenance.

Appropriate aromatic oils would be patchouli, myrrh, peppermint and ginger, which correspond to the angelic spheres of expressive energy, clarity, abundance and prosperous endeavour.

Writing the Blessing

Before starting work on your blessing scroll, you will have assembled and blessed your materials, prayed to Brigid and Michael and intoned the Supplication to the Celtic Deities. Now intone the Rune of Intent:

'As I, (say your name), inscribe this scroll, I affirm that my act is holy, my heart pure, and my words vessels which I pray will be filled and blessed with the power of valiant Michael, Brightness of the Mountains, and Brigid of the Mantle, she who dwells in the golden heart of the sun. May Brigid and Michael bless and protect me and the work that I seek to achieve.'

Then write the Blessing:

'Spirit, give of thine abundance;
Blessed mother of all,
Rock the cradle of this endeavour;
On the goodness of thy milk may it thrive;
In the goodness of earth may it root;

Towards the purity of the stars may it grow.
Spirit, give of thine abundance.

Azara, Butator, in robes of heaven
Like the flame of the sun in its westering,
Bless this endeavour.
Anauel in holy blue,
Enfold it in your rich benediction.
Tual of strength,
Give it your power.
Barakiel of shining goodness,
Add to it your gifts.
Pyrhea of the rubescent living wine,
Kindle its potencies.

Cathonic of the deepest mystery,
Make manifest every dimension of its potential.
Spirit, give of thy abundance
Blessed mother of all.'

(Note that in addition to the Blessing, you will also write the Supplication to the Celtic Deities and a one-line prayer to Brigid and Michael, both overleaf in italic type.)

Intone the Prayer to Brigid and Michael:

'In the name of Brigid the Shining One,
In the name of the Great Chief,
I ask that my prayer for blessing be heard.
I ask that you purify my intention
And make my mind a mountain pool of clarity,
The fish in it leaping and silver

To summon the brightness of the blessing
From the hills of the angels.

May the Archangel Michael, and Brigid the Radiant
In whom dwells the presence of Divine Mother,
Of their benevolence,
Hear and grant my prayer.
By Brigid, by the Great Chief of the Angels, may it be so.'

Write the Supplication to the Celtic Deities (inserting the name
of the recipient if you are not making the scroll for yourself):

'Brigid of the lustre of the stars,
Of the heavenly fire;
Brigid, giver of all good things,
Of your bounty and benevolence,
Breathe the blessed need-fire
Into the heart of my endeavour.

Bran, of noble countenance,
Bran of strength immeasurable,
Look kindly on this enterprise
And let no harm encroach on it.

Epona, of the energies of the earth,
Epona of the bright and lovely forces,
Channel your goodness into this endeavour,
Bless it with the full measure of your potencies.'

Finish the scroll by writing the words:

'By Brigid and by Michael, Great Chief of the Angels, may it be so.'

Now you can decorate the scroll as you wish, before secreting the full-length scroll and displaying a shortened version (if made).

SHORTENED BLESSING FOR THE DISPLAY SCROLL

'Blessed mother of all,
Rock the cradle of this endeavour;
On the goodness of thy milk may it thrive;
In the goodness of earth may it root;
Towards the purity of the stars may it grow.
Spirit, give of thine abundance.

Azara, Butator, in robes of heaven,
Bless this endeavour.
Anauel in holy blue,
Enfold it in your rich benediction.
Tual of strength,
Give it your power.
Barakiel of shining goodness,
Add to it your gifts.
Pyreah of the rubescent living wine,
Kindle its potencies.

Cathonic of the deepest mystery,
Make manifest every dimension of its potential.

Spirit, give of thy abundance
Blessed mother of all.'

7
BLESSING SCROLL
FOR FINDING LOST THINGS

This blessing scroll can be used to find precious lost objects (a wedding ring, for instance), or it can be used to bless the retrieval of a lost pet or even a missing person. Where a pet or a person is involved, it is important to craft the Blessing Scroll for Protection by a Guardian Angel (see page 68) on their behalf as well as this one.

The Angels

Tuthiel, the Angel Over Lost Things, has a bright, hovering appearance, like the radiant shimmer of a supernatural humming bird fanning the ethers as she seeks to perform her services in an ecstasy of joy. Attune to her beautiful, rapidly vibrating energy so that she may lift you into the consciousness of her compassion and her swiftness of response to your plight. When you sense these qualities, Tuthiel can enact them to greater advantage.

She is accompanied by Rochel, who darts like a silver fish in a stream. His eyes are bright and kindly, encompassing every direction simultaneously.

If you have lost a pet, also call on the angel Hariel, gentle brooding angel of domestic animals. His colours are soft earth colours, like the golden falling leaves of autumn and the rich duns of loam. (The angel Tubiel, sweet-voiced and of a silvery, subtle appearance, will call lost birds home.)

If a person is missing, call on the angel of grace, Ananchel, who exudes a healing silence and who wears many radiant crowns from which flow a multitude of blessings. Include the angel of lost souls, Remiel, who flies through lonely and desolate places trailing a symbolic starry net with which he catches up wandering humans into heavenly light.

If a child is missing, petition the angels over lost things (Tuthiel and Rochel) as well as Ananchel and Remiel, and include Afriel, the children's angel. Additionally, call on the angels of mercy, who are Michael, Shekinah, Raphael, Zadkiel and Gabriel. It is a good idea also to call separately on Zadkiel in company with Hasdiel, who together are the angels of benevolence. Also call on Haurvatat (Hower-vah-tet), the great angel, feminine in aspect, who is the personification of salvation. Her heart centre is a perfect rose that shines like a star, and emits the fragrance of paradise, which indeed can be sensed in the perfume of the rose.

If you find it acceptable to call on the saints, it is worth noting that Saint Anthony is renowned for his power of recovering lost things.

When you call on Brigid and Michael during the crafting of this scroll, ask specifically for their protection of the person or animal involved, as well as their blessing.

In all instances, authority must be handed over to the invoked angels. If you can quieten your mind, control your anxieties and pass the task of retrieval to the angels, they will be able to respond much more readily.

The Celtic Deity
⊕ *Brigid*

In all cases of loss, petition Brigid of Brightness: Woman of Compassion, Woman of Healing and Woman of Protection, to help you. Known as Brigid the White in the western isles, she calls all her children home into her pure sheepfolds (see pages 45–46).

Decoration Ideas
Whether you want to decorate a shortened scroll for display purposes or a full-length scroll for secretion, here are some ideas to inspire you.

The image of a shepherd's crook or crozier would be appropriate for this scroll, as a depiction or made in miniature and attached. St Anthony's symbols, which are a Tau cross (T) with a bell fastened on the right arm of the top bar, and a pig (denoting regenerated leadership and direction), would also be helpful.

The names of the Three Magi are connected with the discovery of lost things and missing people. To essay this charm, procure a piece of white wax, melt it in an oven and pour it into just the centres of two small saucers to make two little wax medallions.

Wait until the wax has set smooth and firm, then, with a nail or scissor-tips or any other sharp instrument, inscribe the names of the Magi, which are: Caspar ('white'), Melchoir ('light') and Baltasar ('Lord of the Treasure House') onto both medallions. Slip one into a sandwich bag, then put it under your pillow, and affix the other one to the scroll. Magical tradition says that you will dream of the whereabouts of whatever or whoever you have lost. According to occult lore, attaching the wax saucer to the scroll constitutes an act of protection for what is lost until it is able to be recovered.

For the angels, their protection is signified by these symbols:

⊕ *Tuthiel:* feathers
⊕ *Rochel:* a fish with golden eyes emitting sun rays
⊕ *Hariel:* a golden tree
⊕ *Tubiel:* a small many-coloured bird
⊕ *Ananchel:* a bright crown encircled with a ring of white doves
⊕ *Remiel:* his net of stars
⊕ *Afriel:* pearls, wheat ears and white rose petals
⊕ *Angels of Mercy:* a pot of balm
⊕ *Angels of Benevolence:* a cornucopia
⊕ *Haurvatat:* a rose emitting light

For the Celtic deity, her sign is:

⊕ *Brigid*: an equal-sided cross of light within a ring of light

Suitable crystals would be 'diamond-window' clear quartz point and tumbled tiger iron, which respectively link to the angelic spheres of far sight and the provision of sanctuary.

Appropriate aromatic oils would be frankincense, which corresponds to the angelic spheres of stability, security and consolation, and rose.

Writing the Blessing

Before starting work on your blessing scroll, you will have assembled and blessed your materials, prayed to Brigid and Michael and intoned the Supplication to the Celtic Deities. Now intone the Rune of Intent:

'As I, (say your name), inscribe this scroll, I affirm that my act is holy, my heart pure, and my words vessels which I pray will be filled and blessed with the power of valiant Michael, Brightness of the Mountains, and Brigid of the Mantle, she who dwells in the golden heart of the sun. May Brigid and Michael bless and protect me and the work that I seek to achieve.'

Then write the Blessing (but see variations opposite):

'Tuthiel, bright-hearted, melodious-mouthed,
Voice of loveliness beyond reed or harp,
O Angel over Lost Things,
Give forth thy sweet summoning call,
Unite me again with what I desire to see.

Rochel, Gatherer-In,
Ananchel of Grace,
Thou five angels of mercy,
Thou angels of brimming benevolence,
Haurvatat of Salvation,
Of the Presence of the Rose,
Remiel of the starry net,
Thou angel of lost souls,
Call the wandering one home.
For the one whom my heart is calling,
I intone this blessing:

The safeguard of Brigid round your feet;
Whole be your return home;
Be the bright Michael king of the angels,
Protecting, and keeping, and saving you.
The guarding of God of All be yours,
Till I or mine shall see you again.

And the peace-giving Spirit, everlasting, be yours,
The peace-giving Spirit, everlasting, be yours.'

If you are seeking lost objects, intone and write the first verse only, followed by the first line of the second verse conjoined with the last line of the first verse (this is all that is necessary for inanimate things:

'Tuthiel, bright-hearted, melodious-mouthed,
Voice of loveliness beyond reed or harp,
O Angel over Lost Things,
Give forth thy sweet summoning call,
Unite me again with what I desire to see.

Rochel, Gatherer-In,
Unite me again with what I desire to see.'

If you are seeking an animal, intone and write the entire set of verses, adding Angel Hariel (and Tubiel if appropriate) to the angels petitioned in the second verse. Angel Hariel is a comforting presence that will be sensed by your lost animal companion.

(Note that in addition to the Blessing, you will also write the Supplication to the Celtic Deities and a one-line prayer to Brigid and Michael, both overleaf in italic type.)

Intone the Prayer to Brigid and Michael:

'In the name of Brigid the Shining One,
In the name of the Great Chief,
I ask that my prayer for blessing be heard.
I ask that you purify my intention
And make my mind a mountain pool of clarity,
The fish in it leaping and silver
To summon the brightness of the blessing
From the hills of the angels.

May the Archangel Michael, and Brigid the Radiant
In whom dwells the presence of Divine Mother,
Of their benevolence,
Hear and grant my prayer.
By Brigid, by the Great Chief of the Angels, may it be so.'

Write the Supplication to the Celtic Deity:

'Brigid of Brightness, Brigid the White,
Hear my prayer, O Woman of Compassion.
Brigid of the pure sheepfolds,
Brigid, Shepherdess,
Call the lost home;
Call my loved one home.'

Finish the scroll by writing the words:

'By Brigid, by the Great Chief of the Angels, may it be so.'

Now you can decorate the scroll as you wish, before secreting the full-length scroll and displaying a shortened version of the scroll (if made) using the wording below.

SHORTENED BLESSING FOR THE DISPLAY SCROLL

'Tuthiel, bright-hearted, melodious-mouthed,
Voice of loveliness beyond reed or harp,
O Angel over Lost Things,
Give forth thy sweet summoning call,
Unite me again with what I desire to see.

Rochel, Gatherer-In,
Ananchel of Grace,
Thou five angels of mercy,
Thou angels of brimming benevolence,
Haurvatat of Salvation,
Of the Presence of the Rose,
Remiel of the starry net,
Thou angel of lost souls,
Call the wandering one home.'

8

BLESSING SCROLL
FOR
A NEW HOME

T his scroll can be used when moving into a new home, or at any time during its occupation. A building, particularly a dwelling, begins to form a soul as soon as its foundation is laid. This soul (a blend of all the influences infused into it) can be cleansed and attuned anew to the soul emanations of its occupants. Thus a welcoming atmosphere and nurturing energies are assured.

The Angels

The angels of the home are led by the protective angel Nihangius ('Ny-an-gyus').

However, each home has its own guardian angel. By attuning to your own angel of the home, you will be able to discover its personal name. Just ask as you sit in peace and communion. The first name that comes clearly to your mind will be that of the angel presiding over your home.

Nihangius embraces both masculine and feminine aspects. She draws near to bless each task performed in the home, and, where she is allowed, breathes an atmosphere of reassurance, warmth and safety into the domestic interior. The masculine principle within Nihangius tends to safeguard the exterior of the home, and draws attention to the need for repairs and maintenance, inspiring the urge to tackle such jobs. Both aspects conjoin to infuse a charge of love and a devotion to spiritual principles into the ambience of the home, and to bless the occupants' choice of colours and decoration. They will strive to ensure that these choices embrace the enhancement of an interior that is in keeping with the soul needs and development of their human charges, for the angels of the home work with our guardian angels to safeguard our wellbeing and spiritual progress. Colour, in particular, embodies spritual qualities to which the individual soul attunes and resonates according to its development.

The angel of the home, like all the angels, loves to be given tasks. If you cannot think of how to accommodate things into adequate storage space, or you are confronted with a seemingly hopeless muddle, you need have no idea before you begin as to how you will solve the problem. Simply start the job, and call on the angel of the home to lend its assistance. You will be surprised by how enthusiastic and inspired you will become as the angel takes its post within you and begins joyfully to direct operations!

It revels in lending angelic grace and very practical assistance, in the sense of inspiration and positive energy, to such dreary situations. Everything falls into place and you feel like an artist rather than a drudge

This is the great aspiration of the angel of the home – to bring to the most mundane, unprepossessing, dirty tasks a sense of the sublime, a sense of paradise, so that we feel that we are communing with a vast brotherhood to bless life in all its dimensions as we work. The angel of the home seeks to lift us away from the arena of chores and drudgery, from domestic exasperation and constriction, to a realization that it is the centre, the hearth or heart, with which we deal when we are in our homes, and that within them we objectify our deeper self. The angel of the home ever strives to create sanctuary, a link with the higher worlds, within our homes, so that they become our own sacred circle or kirk. It seeks to enable us to express the profoundest essence of our spirit via simple, humble, everyday procedures, and build within the home a citadel of happiness, security and love that in itself emits a blessing. Whether you summon the angel of the home with the intention of making a blessing scroll for yourself or for others, it is helpful to bear these things in mind as you enter into communion with it.

The Celtic Deities
⊕ Brigid
⊕ Columba

Brigid is all-encompassing, the goddess of infinitude and worlds without end, yet she is also the presiding goddess over hearth and home. There are many beautiful blessings originating from the Hebrides (a system of islands that bear a version of her name – Bride – within their own name) that poignantly express this truth: the kitchen blessing, the churning blessing, the hearth blessing, the hatching blessing and the blessing for a child in its cradle. Brigid enshrines the sacred feminine, and shows us that even while it ministers to the smallest details, it is limitless in its breadth, scope and integrative vision.

Columba was a saint of the Scottish Western Isles who was so venerated that he was virtually given the status of a deity by the isles-folk. He was born a prince in Ireland, but devoted himself to a religious life from such an early age that he was known as Columncille ('Column of the cell'). He was baptized with two names: Crimthian ('wolf') and Columba ('dove'). He had a fierce warrior nature, and had to strive hard to bring all its aspects under the control and into the service of his spiritual principles. Ultimately, the dove was triumphant.

Columba came under the divine tutelage of Brigid, mystical Woman of Compassion, and so great was his own compassion that he would often shed tears at the distress of the country people to whom he ministered. He was a great scholar and musician, and a tender protector of animals. Of his singing it was said in an old bardic poem: 'The sound of his voice/Great is its sweetness above every company.'

Columba settled on Iona with his following of monks, and devoted himself to a life of altruistic love and spiritual service. Today, the island is magically endowed with the grace of his presence. He espoused Christian teachings, but it is clear from the way in which he was remembered in the Hebrides that he also respected the old religion of the people. He often provided them with charms and runes to solve their problems. Many of them saw a light shining around his head, and said of him that 'he had the face of an angel, and although on earth, seemed to be living in heaven'. When he died, it was reported that he was 'wonderfully gladdened by visions of holy angels coming to greet him'.

Columba was a humble man, despite his princely and warrior status. He sublimated his arrogance and transformed it into compassion. He gave equally devout attention to the problem of a peasant woman whose cow could not bring forth her calf, or whose kitchen needed blessing, as he did to the coronation of kings at which he was the presiding officiant. Like Brigid, he attended to the care of humble, domestic concerns as well as to those of immense magnitude.

Decoration Ideas

Whether you want to decorate a shortened scroll for display purposes or a full-length scroll for secretion, here are some ideas to inspire you.

Red thread is suitable for this blessing scroll, as is the image of an umbrella, a symbol of heavenly shelter, which is considered a mascot of great power, bringing domestic bliss and universal good fortune. It is venerated as one of the Eight Glorious Emblems of Buddha. (In Eastern countries, the umbrella has been a component of the insignia of royalty and a symbol of state and power since the founding of civilization, where it was first known as the Canopy of State.)

A wonderful emblem for this blessing scroll is Brigid's Cross, which is traditionally woven from grasses or reeds. It takes the form of a saltire or St Andrew's Cross (X) with a square at its centre, representing spiritual power emanating from stability. The trefoil is the herb that has been designated as the Sign of Column, and is equally appropriate.

Natural items from the kitchen and garden can be used to decorate this scroll. Houseleek and ivy are particularly fortunate with respect to the home, as are lavender and rosemary. Variegated ivy symbolizes angelic protection, whilst green ivy shields from storms and lightning damage.

For the angel, his protection is signified by these symbols:

⊕ *Nihangius:* a pair of encircling arms, and a hearth fire surrounded by angels

For the Celtic deities, their shared sign is:

⊕ *Columba and Brigid:* a dove (symbolizing the sanctuary of the home)

A suitable crystal would be an emerald, the jewel associated with the heart of the rainbow, which links to the angelic spheres of the heart, domestic bliss, inspiration and harmony.

Appropriate aromatic oils would be frankincense, which corresponds to the angelic spheres of stability and security, and rose, which corresponds to the angelic spheres of sanctuary and love.

Writing the Blessing

Before starting work on your blessing scroll, you will have assembled and blessed your materials, prayed to Brigid and Michael and intoned the Supplication to the Celtic Deities. Now intone the Rune of Intent:

'As I, (say your name), inscribe this scroll, I affirm that my act is holy, my heart pure, and my words vessels which I pray will be filled and blessed with the power of valiant Michael, Brightness of the Mountains, and Brigid of the Mantle, she who dwells in the golden heart of the sun. May Brigid and Michael bless and protect me and the work that I seek to achieve.'

Then write the Blessing:

'God, give charge to your blessed angels
To keep guard around this house by day and night;

A band consecrated, hearty and brave,
That will shield this soul-shrine from harm.
Nihangius, Encircling One,
Angel of the hearth and home;
Host of brightest angels bringing blessing,
Bless thou this house,
From site to stay,
From beam to wall,
From end to end,
From ridge to basement,
From balk to tree-roof,
From foundation to summit.
Foundation and summit,
Blessed be.

We see the host upon the wing;
We see sunwise rings of purest brightness;
We see angels move around the house
In sunwise rings of purest brightness.'

(Note that in addition to the Blessing, you will also write the Supplication to the Celtic Deities and a one-line prayer to Brigid and Michael, both below in italic type.)

Intone the Prayer to Brigid and Michael:

'In the name of Brigid the Shining One,
In the name of the Great Chief,
I ask that my prayer for blessing be heard.
I ask that you purify my intention
And make my mind a mountain pool of clarity,
The fish in it leaping and silver

To summon the brightness of the blessing
From the hills of the angels.
May the Archangel Michael, and Brigid the Radiant
In whom dwells the presence of Divine Mother,
Of their benevolence,
Hear and grant my prayer.
By Brigid, by the Great Chief of the Angels, may it be so.'

Write the Supplication to the Celtic Deities:

'The encompassment of Brigid,
Bride of the golden hair,
Guarding the hearth, guarding the door,
Guarding the household all.

Who are they on the lawn without?
Brigid, most lovely flower of fire,
Michael the sun-radiant of our trust.
Who are they within the door?
Bright angels of protection and blessing.
Who are they by the front of the bed?
Sun-bright Mary and the Son of Peace.

The mouth of God ordained,
The angel of God proclaimed,
An angel white in charge of the hearth
Till white day shall come to the embers.
An angel white in charge of the hearth
Till white day shall come to the embers.

Columba, beneficent, benign,
The cross of the saints and the angels

Down over this house
From foundation to summit
By thy grace;
And thou, melodious-mouth'd,
Chanting your blessings upon it,
The joyous blessing of thy mouth
Falling in blessing upon it.'

Finish the scroll by writing the words:

'By Brigid, by the Great Chief of the Angels, may it be so.'

Now you can decorate the scroll as you wish, before secreting the full-length scroll and displaying a shortened version of the scroll (if made) using the wording opposite.

SHORTENED BLESSING FOR THE DISPLAY SCROLL

'God, give charge to your blessed angels
To keep guard around this house by day and night;
A band consecrated, hearty and brave,
That will shield this soul-shrine from harm.

Nihangius, Encircling One,
Angel of the hearth and home;
Host of brightest angels bringing blessing,
Bless thou this house,
From site to stay,
From beam to wall,
From end to end,
From ridge to basement,
From balk to tree-roof,
From foundation to summit.
Foundation and summit,
Blessed be.'

9
BLESSING SCROLL
FOR A BRIDE

This blessing scroll, which incorporates the bridegroom in its compass, can be made for a couple at any time in their marriage as well as being presented to a bride on her wedding day. Ideally this should done before the wedding takes place, although there is no hard and fast rule. The scroll can easily be adapted to include same-sex marriages.

The Angels

The angels attending a marriage blessing are numerous. As well as your own guardian angel (see Blessing Scroll for Protection by a Guardian Angel), they include the angels of love: Shekinah, Raphael, Theliel, Rahmiel, Donquel, Itkal and Anael; the angels of peace, led by Gabriel and Valohel; the angels of protection, led by Michael; the angel of friendship, who is Mihr; the angel of the home, who is Nihangius; the angel of fidelity, who is Mihael; the angel of marriage, who is Omniel; the angel of domestic harmony, who is Camaysar; the angel of fertility, of inspiration and the gifting of inspiration one to one another, who is Samandiriel; the angel of sexual joy and devotion, who is Rachiel; the angel of our own individual uniqueness as an expression of love, presided over by Liwet; the angel of liberation and independence within the framework of committed relationships, presided over by Shekinah; the angel of abundance, who is Barbelo; and the angel of new beginnings, renewal and enlightenment, who is Gazardiel, the beautiful angel of the dawn.

This is rather an exhausting list, so the best way to summon these angels might simply be to imagine the couple under a rose bower (a sacred place of unification for lovers), and then to call on the angels one by one, contemplating the virtues and gifts they offer and seeing them being given in abundance to both the bride and bridegroom. See the essence of these marvellous gifts surrounding the pair in a ring of angelic light and joy. This is the true wedding ring, which also signifies fidelity and eternity.

Your ability to feel the wonder and the happiness of these gifts as they are bestowed will open up a magnificent conduit for the use of the angels. It may be that you sense fragrances and colours. In the case of the angels of love, for instance, you might note that each angel gives forth a differing quality of love, which you may see as a range of colours changing in hue.

Call on the angels of love as a whole as well as the named angels, and similarly for the angels of peace and also the angels of protection.

The Celtic Deities
⊕ *Brigid*
⊕ *Bran*
⊕ *Morgan*

Brigid, goddess of purity and all-encompassing love, is the perfect goddess to preside over a wedding. The word 'bride' is derived from her name. She blesses, inspires, and forges soundly in holy fire the configurations of spirit that comprise lifelong commitment, dedication and joy.

Bran stands stalwart and steadfast over the soul-shrine of the marrying couple, driving away by a mighty word of command the savage wolves and searing shadows that seek to threaten a happy and loyal union.

Morgan, direly misunderstood in our folklore, is the essence of the Sacred Marriage, and stands surety for it.

Decoration Ideas
Whether you want to decorate a shortened scroll for display purposes or a full-length scroll for secretion, here are some ideas to inspire you.

There are numerous ways to enhance this scroll. Allow your imagination to take flight without reservation! You might decide on the traditional 'something old, something new, something borrowed, something blue' theme for part of it. Rosebuds and pearls are symbolic of the start of a marriage. Small pieces of clear quartz denote protection and positive potential, whilst pieces of rose quartz signify love and devotion.

You may choose to study the language of flowers (a Victorian method of communicating via flowers, which were all given their different meanings) to inspire your thoughts on decoration. Here are some of the flowers and their meanings:

⊕ *apple blossom:* fecundity, beauty and goodness
⊕ *bay leaves and bluebells:* constancy
⊕ *buttercup:* radiant happiness
⊕ *carnation (white):* devotion
⊕ *dandelion and rowan berries:* tokens of Brigid
⊕ *feverfew:* 'Let me shield you.'
⊕ *myrtle:* love's fragrance, 'Be mine forever.'
⊕ *orange blossom:* happy marriage
⊕ *pink:* 'No matter what the years may bring, for me your beauty will never die.'
⊕ *rose (full-blown red rose):* the heart's mystery and the perfection of love; an emblem of the angel of the star of love
⊕ *tiger lily:* 'My passion burns like a firebrand.'
⊕ *veronica*: true love, 'Nothing shall ever part us.'

Old jewellery might be used to depict treasures in store, especially the spiritual significance of the ring (the unbroken circle), whilst angel wings, hearts and doves symbolize blessings. The lovers' knot is a sign of fidelity and unbroken union, and horseshoes, birdhouses and black cats all depict fertility blessings and good luck.

Of all the angels, Shekinah and the angels of love (who are expressions of one another) suggest themselves as the supreme influences for the decoration of this scroll. Archangel Michael is the male aspect and the mirror reflection of Shekinah, and is ever present within her, as she is within him. (As always, if you think differently, go with your feelings.)

For the angels, their protection is signified by these symbols:

- ⊕ *angels of love:* a full-blown rose
- ⊕ *angels of peace:* a white dove descending
- ⊕ *angels of protection:* a sword of light
- ⊕ *Nihangius (angel of the home):* a hearth fire surrounded by angels
- ⊕ *Mihr (angel of friendship):* a jewelled cave
- ⊕ *Mihael (angel of fidelity):* a ring or a pair of swans
- ⊕ *Omniel (angel of marriage):* a lovers' knot
- ⊕ *Camaysar (angel of domestic harmony):* encircling arms
- ⊕ *Samandiriel (angel of fertility):* an orb reflecting stars
- ⊕ *Rachiel (angel of sexual joy):* a flame
- ⊕ *Liwet (angel of individual uniqueness):* a clear gemstone reflecting a rainbow
- ⊕ *Shekinah (angel of independence within a relationship):* an ascending golden bird
- ⊕ *Barbelo (angel of abundance):* a celestial spring with a flow of gold down to Earth
- ⊕ *Gazardiel (angel of beginnings):* the rising sun

For the Celtic deities, their signs are:

- ⊕ *Brigid:* pearls and a blue hyacinth
- ⊕ *Bran:* a great door sealed with the sign of the cross of light within a ring of light
- ⊕ *Morgan:* a golden jewelled loving cup (with a handle on both sides)

Suitable crystals would be a diamond (said to enhance the love of a husband for his wife), rose quartz and clear quartz, which correspond to the angelic spheres of love, devotion and the Sacred Marriage, which is the perfectly balanced interplay of the life forces.

Appropriate aromatic oils would be rose, which links us to the angelic spheres of the mystery of love, ylang-ylang, and spikenard, which corresponds to the angelic sphere of the sacred marriage. This rare and costly oil, which is spoken of in the Bible in connection with the Queen of Sheba and Mary Magdalene, signifies the union between heaven and Earth, and is traditionally applied to the head and the feet.

Writing the Blessing

Before starting work on your blessing scroll, you will have assembled and blessed your materials, prayed to Brigid and Michael and intoned the Supplication to the Celtic Deities. Now intone the Rune of Intent:

'As I, (say your name), inscribe this scroll, I affirm that my act is holy, my heart pure, and my words vessels which I pray will be filled and blessed with the power of valiant Michael, Brightness of the Mountains, and Brigid of the Mantle, she who dwells in the golden heart of the sun. May Brigid and Michael bless and protect me and the work that I seek to achieve.'

Then write the Blessing (omitting the penultimate line of the second verse if the word 'parenting' is inappropriate for this blessing scroll):

'On this day of days,
The bright morning of your hope,
The high noon-tide of your happiness,
The fair evening of your joy,
The starry night of your new sheltering,
May you be blessed
By the highest host of heaven

With the nine joys,
And with the blessing of the Three
Who fill the heights.
The angels of love
To light your soul-shrine;
The angels of peace
To bestow soul serenity;
The angels of protection
To encompass and shield you,
The angels of friendship
To keep you in fair havens;
The angels of ecstasy
To bind your two bodies;
The angels of the heart's tenderness
To keep you in constancy;
The angels of the bliss of silence
To keep you in heart communion;
The angels of abundance
To keep want from your door;
And the gifts of shining Samandiriel
To bring you joy of parenting
And bright potency of living.

The joy of the rose of Mary be in your chamber;
The joy of the fullness of Brigid be in your kitchen;
The joy of the graces be around your hearth;
The joy of the wide world be ever encompassing and blessing
your union.'

(Note that in addition to the Blessing, you will also write the Supplication to the Celtic Deities and a one-line prayer to Brigid and Michael, opposite and overleaf in italic type.)

Intone the Prayer to Brigid and Michael:

'In the name of Brigid the Shining One,
In the name of the Great Chief,
I ask that my prayer for blessing be heard.
I ask that you purify my intention
And make my mind a mountain pool of clarity,
The fish in it leaping and silver
To summon the brightness of the blessing
From the hills of the angels.
May the Archangel Michael, and Brigid the Radiant
In whom dwells the presence of Divine Mother,
Of their benevolence,
Hear and grant my prayer.
By Brigid, by the Great Chief of the Angels, may it be so.'

Write the Supplication to the Celtic Deities (changing the wording of the first verse to: 'Bless this bridegroom in his joy,/Bless the bride who greets him.' if the scroll is for the groom):

'Brigid of the bright countenance,
Brigid of the goodness of all things,
Bless this bride in her joy,
Bless the bridegroom who attends her,
Bless this day of days,
And bless this marriage throughout each moment of its span.

Bran of the strength of mountains,
Bran of the stalwartness of stone,
Set to flight all that would harm this union;
Keep within its containment
Every blessing and joy that it receives in its heart.

Morgan, exalted One of the Mysteries,
Give this marriage the blessing
Of your sublime essence,
The supreme nectar of excellence
That transforms and transcends.'

Finish the scroll by writing the words:

'By Brigid, by the Great Chief of the Angels, may it be so.'

Now you can decorate the scroll as you wish, before secreting the full-length scroll and displaying a shortened version of the scroll (if made) using the wording opposite.

SHORTENED BLESSING FOR THE DISPLAY SCROLL

'On this day of days,
The bright morning of your hope,
The high noon-tide of your happiness,
The starry night of your new sheltering,
May you be blessed
By the highest host of heaven.

The angels of love
To light your soul-shrine;
The angels of protection
To encompass and shield you;
The angels of friendship
To keep you in fair havens;
The angels of ecstasy
To bind your two bodies;
The angels of the heart's tenderness
To keep you in constancy;
The angels of the bliss of silence
To keep you in heart communion;
And the gifts of shining Samandiriel
To bring you bright potency of living.'

10

BLESSING SCROLL
FOR TURNING AN ENEMY INTO A FRIEND

This blessing scroll can also be used to supplicate healing for an ailing friendship, work relationship or love relationship, or to heal relations between family members. In severe cases, it may be necessary to create the Blessing Scroll for Healing (see page 180) alongside this one. Where only one party wants to make amends, address the highest essence of both individuals in your blessing.

The Angels

The angels of blessing are Shekinah, Barakiel and Phanuel, Jophiel, Lelahel and Hasdiel, Zadkiel, Hael and Hahaiah, and Gabriel and the Virtues.

Although they appear in differing guises according to the requirements of different situations, these angels of blessing form a ring of blazing light when they are called upon as a whole. They become a single entity, generating a circuit of spiritual electricity, which infuses its recipient with divine light and eliminates encroaching shadows.

You can elicit their power of blessing to turn an enemy into a friend, as stated, or simply to surround a loved one with the blessing of heavenly light and its forcefield of magical positivity and happiness.

Think of this heavenly light in association with the blessing angels as a ray of bright white light, gentle to the eyes yet shining with a brilliance beyond that of earthly light; as a cascade of golden light like a sunburst, yet with a depth of richness and sublimity in its goldenness that is heavenly and angelic; and as a starry outpouring of clear light like an emission of flashes from a celestial diamond of surpassing purity and vividness of essence. The fourth aspect of this light is the radiance of the rainbow.

As you enter into these differing qualities of the light of heaven and think of the angels of grace and blessing, you will naturally summon them and come into their presence. See yourself at the heart of their magical ring, and, by intoning the person's name, call upon the soul of the recipient of the blessing scroll to take their place at the centre of the circle.

If you are supplicating the angels of blessing in order to turn an enemy into a friend, call also upon Baglis, Colopatiron, Balthial, Chamuel, Gavreel, Mihr, Itkal and, in a separate instance from those named above, Phanuel.

Baglis is the angel of temperance. She restores emotional balance and tenderly resurrects and heals a fractured will. She teaches us to use our will with gentle, relaxed persistence rather than aiming to employ it as a battering ram, from which ill-advised exercise we often fall back exhausted, undermined and helpless. If there is an element of addiction at any level in the feelings of enmity that have arisen, Baglis will loosen its claws, hooks and tentacles and transform it into a dynamic tenacity of focus resolved on addressing the problem and restoring equilibrium. Simultaneously, Baglis gentles the intensity of that inner focus.

Colopatiron is the angel who unlocks prison doors. Whenever we find ourselves locked into a situation as if chained within imprisoning walls of negativity, Colopatiron will come at our summons to release us from our incarceration, bearing the solvent of divine love as his key. He is the angel of freedom.

Balthial lifts us above feelings of jealousy and resentment, calming the furies that rage in our psyche with an upheld hand of blessing emanating celestial power from the highest angelic realms. He surrounds us with the healing balm of forgiveness, allowing us to forgive ourselves and others. His gifts are centredness, loving tolerance and peace of mind. Where there are troubled waves seething through the psyche, Balthial clears the storm and pours forth an essence of tranquillity that soothes and stills.

Chamuel works with Balthial to nurture tolerance in our hearts and to engender love for ourselves so that we can truly love others. When we judge ourselves kindly and gently, we find we can drop sniping, judgmental attitudes towards others. Chamuel eases tense, distressed stances deep within the human psyche.

Gavreel works with Balthial and Chamuel, forming with them a trinity of angelic harmony. Gavreel is the angel of reconciliation, who helps us to make peace with our enemies. A perfect spiritual equilibrium is his gift of blessing.

Mihr is the beautiful angel of friendship, who casts his soft glow of harmonious love, helping us to delight in another's company and appreciate the many wonders of their being, as if we were looking into a jewelled cavern.

Itkal throws off bright circles of harmony and tranquillity. He inspires co-operation and affection, and fosters harmonious relationships. He pours angelic balm on troubled waters.

Phanuel is the angel of hope and joy, who shines like a bright golden star. Brilliantly radiant, she brings gifts of surpassing happiness, beauty and perfect heart-attunement within her healing wings. When a dull landscape, lifeless and featureless, suddenly lights up with the golden radiance of the sun and is filled with an instant beauty that gladdens the heart, Phanuel is drawing close to the earth planes. What we see in outward expression is the joy and the beauty that Phanuel can bring to our lives when we open ourselves to her lovely influences.

Chant the names of these angels of forgiveness, reconciliation and joy, summoning and supplicating them to be present as you make your blessing scroll and to lend their aid to your purpose. You may wish to continue working with these angels for a few weeks after your scroll is complete to ensure that the troubled psychic conditions surrounding the situation are completely healed.

The Celtic Deities

⊕ *Brigid*
⊕ *Bran*
⊕ *Columba*

Brigid, goddess of the mind, body and spirit that comprise each one of us, is the ideal divine influence to call upon for blessings and reconciliation. She emanates and bestows the white light of perfect peace, of heavenly magic that turns our lives to gold.

135

Bran, huge and four-square, will stand no nonsense and brook no resistance from the adversarial forces that try to block, hinder and darken our resolution to forgive, heal and centre ourselves in blessing, in the god forces.

Columba, who struggled at first with his own tendencies to retaliate and bear grudges, is a wonderful human example of how we can gloriously overcome our lower selves. He will lend every aid to our resolution to bless, to forgive and to heal rifts. He is the dove who gentled the wolf.

Decoration Ideas

Whether you want to decorate a shortened scroll for display purposes or a full-length scroll for secretion, here are some ideas.

There are many emblems of blessing, such as the corn dolly, dove, bee, scarab, olive tree, rowan tree and fir tree. However, in the case of this blessing scroll, it is particularly beneficial to use the images of angels. If you cannot draw or paint them, simply use the découpage method of cutting out and pasting pictures from greetings cards, particularly Christmas cards.

Although you may be calling on the angels of freedom, forgiveness, reconciliation and joy to help you to resolve an unhappy situation, your main focus will be the angels of blessing. White, gold and pastel rainbow tints are ideal for this scroll.

For the angels, their protection is signified by these symbols:
- *a ring of light filled with light*
- *white enfolding wings*
- *upheld hands, palms outward, emitting light*

For the Celtic deities, their signs are:
- *Brigid:* an oyster-catcher (black and white wader with orange beak), pearls, rowan berries

⊕ *Bran:* sage leaves, a crowned head
⊕ *Columba:* a dove

Suitable crystals would be celestite, which links to the highest angelic realms, and carnelian, which corresponds with the angelic spheres of blessing.

Appropriate aromatic oils would be frankincense and rose, both of which help to connect us to the angels of blessing.

Writing the Blessing

Before starting work on your blessing scroll, you will have assembled and blessed your materials, prayed to Brigid and Michael and intoned the Supplication to the Celtic Deities. Now intone the Rune of Intent:

'As I, (say your name), inscribe this scroll, I affirm that my act is holy, my heart pure, and my words vessels which I pray will be filled and blessed with the power of valiant Michael, Brightness of the Mountains, and Brigid of the Mantle, she who dwells in the golden heart of the sun. May Brigid and Michael bless and protect me and the work that I seek to achieve.'

Then write the Blessing. As this blessing is intoned and inscribed, it is important to sail above any inharmonious feelings or sense of discord. Give your all in blessing and goodwill as you direct this magical force to the recipient of the scroll, because the angels work with what we give them. Add your light and purpose to that of the angels, and your blessing will soar above the clouds of the earth plane and shine a brilliance from above that will melt away the tight knot of grievance that has formed itself between you and the person who bears you ill will. Healing begins immediately, and both of you will feel its balm before you meet again.

If you are making the scroll to bestow a general blessing, work in the same way. Even though in this case you will not need to call on the second group of angels listed, take a little time to focus specifically on Phanuel. Phanuel and Gabriel, of all the angels that comprise the circle of blessing, tend to draw closest to humanity in their physical incarnation.

'Angels of blessing encompass you,
Angels of blessing ring you round
In whiteness of blessing,
In beauteous gold;
In the white and the gold of Michael and Brigid,
In the white and the gold of the bright angels.

Deep peace may they breathe into you;
Deep peace, a soft white dove to you;
Deep peace, a quiet rain to you;
Deep peace, an ebbing wave to you.

Deep peace, red wind of the east from you;
Deep peace, grey wind of the west to you;
Deep peace, dark wind of the north from you;
Deep peace, blue wind of the south to you.
Deep peace, pure red of the flame to you;
Deep peace, pure white of the moon to you;
Deep peace, pure green of the grass to you;
Deep peace, pure brown of the earth to you.

Deep peace, pure grey of the dew to you;
Deep peace, pure blue of the sky to you;
Deep peace of the running wave to you;
Deep peace of the flowing air to you.

Deep peace of the quiet earth to you;
Deep peace of the sleeping stones to you;
Deep peace of the Golden Shepherd to you;
Deep peace of the White Shepherdess to you.

Deep peace of the Flock of Stars to you;
Deep peace from the Son of Peace to you;
Deep peace from the heart of Mary to you;
And from Brigid of the Mantle,
Blessings rich as the foaming milk.

In the name of the Three who are One,
White peace;
And by the will of the King of the Elements
White peace;
Deep peace, and the richness of all blessings be with you
This very hour, and
Throughout the quiet circlings of all your days.'

(Note that in addition to the Blessing, you will also write the Supplication to the Celtic Deities and a one-line prayer to Brigid and Michael, both below in italic type.)

Intone the Prayer to Brigid and Michael:

'In the name of Brigid the Shining One,
In the name of the Great Chief,
I ask that my prayer for blessing be heard.
I ask that you purify my intention
And make my mind a mountain pool of clarity,
The fish in it leaping and silver
To summon the brightness of the blessing

From the hills of the angels.
May the Archangel Michael, and Brigid the Radiant
In whom dwells the presence of Divine Mother,
Of their benevolence,
Hear and grant my prayer.
By Brigid, by the Great Chief of the Angels, may it be so.'

Write the Supplication to the Celtic Deities:

'Brigid of the shining hair,
Of the blue eyes of heaven that bless,
Of the melodious mouth that blesses,
Bring your goodly force to bless my need;
Touch hearts that they may be opened and healed.

Bran the Blessed, warrior of the light,
Protect me and the one I seek to bless;
Night and day
And throughout the shades of twilight
Stand guard at our soul-shrine.

Columba, man of mercy,
Columba, who summoned forth the gentle dove
From the depths of the wolf,
Hear my prayer;

Let flow your healing magic
To heal the wound of this rift
I seek to close.
Let the wound close up and be gone forever
By your godly mercy.'

Finish the scroll by writing the words:

'By Brigid and by Michael, Great Chief of the Angels, may it be so.'

Now you can decorate the scroll as you wish, before secreting the full-length scroll and displaying a shortened version of the scroll (if made) using the wording below.

SHORTENED BLESSING FOR THE DISPLAY SCROLL

'Angels of blessing encompass you,
Angels of blessing ring you round
In whiteness of blessing,
In beauteous gold;

Deep peace may they breathe into you;
Deep peace, a soft white dove to you;
Deep peace, a quiet rain to you;
Deep peace, pure red of the flame to you;
Deep peace, pure white of the moon to you;
Deep peace, pure green of the grass to you;
Deep peace, pure grey of the dew to you;
Deep peace, pure blue of the sky to you;
Deep peace of the running wave to you;
Deep peace of the flowing air to you.
Deep peace of the quiet earth to you;
Deep peace of the Son of Peace to you.

Deep peace, and the richness of all blessings be with you
This very hour,
And throughout the quiet circlings of all your days.'

11

BLESSING SCROLL
FOR PROTECTING A CHILD
DURING PREGNANCY AND BIRTH

This scroll can be used where there is a family history of birthing problems, or simply to give a mother reassurance if she feels trepidation. The angels and deities (which represent natural forces) involved in its creation give forth a wonderful sense of almost palpable shielding and protection, bringing a sense of comfort, reassurance and safety that is calming and healing.

The Angels

The angel Afriel is described as an angel of force, of the supreme power of the heavens. There is a likeness to Archangel Michael in that the divine masculine aspect of this angel shines forth with a mighty radiance, casting bright circles of protection outwards from his heart, which encompass and fortify those who call on him.

Yet at his heart, at his source, is enshrined the divine feminine essence of Afriel. She manifests as a sweetly beautiful black Madonna, bearing a form very much like Isis. At her heart is a six-pointed star, which burns with a coruscating intensity of white-silver light. The star combines the two aspects of the angel in a perfect androgyne. This exquisite being does indeed emanate divine force, sweeping its wings in rhythmic encircling pulses of love, upliftment and protection. Enter this perfect point of attunement, which is both Michael and Afriel, and bathe in its divine power.

Above Afriel stands Brigid, glorious golden one, both angel and goddess, woman of compassion and all-encompassing protection. Adding his light to theirs, Archangel Michael stands as guardian of the spiritual sphere that they inhabit. Beside them stands Sandalphon, great bright angel of the Earth and angel of the embryo, stretching out arms of incandescent power to protect the child you seek to help and add his blessing to that of Brigid, Michael and Afriel.

There is a tenderness, indeed an almost human kindliness, that streams from this angel. Afriel forbids any hurt, any danger to approach the child within the womb and during labour. Melt into the divine gaze of the angel Afriel and carry the idea of the child you wish to protect, the vibration of its soul, deep into that golden radiant world of which the angel's eyes are a manifestation and a portal.

Feel the Michael force and the Brigid-Isis force (there is a very deep connection between these two) of this mighty angel enfold the child in exquisite wings that shield, protect and encircle in a triumph of God's perfect bright-rayed love.

The Celtic Deities

⊕ *Bran*
⊕ *Druantia*
⊕ *Dana*

Bran the Blessed is an ancient British sun deity, to whom the Celts paid tribute for his prophetic skills and his powers of guardianship. His symbol is the raven, considered to be the most intelligent bird species on Earth. He was known as Bran of the Wounded Thighs, and in fact this connects him with the Fisher King, the true Father God, who mourns and bleeds because his beloved consort and source, Divine Mother, has been torn away from him. This marks Bran as one who knows, one who is connected to divine wisdom. He is the all-powerful Father because he understands his oneness with the all-powerful Mother. He has undergone the terrible wounding of the death forces at their most pernicious and has emerged triumphant and whole, filled with the glory of the undiminished sun.

See Bran as a mighty protector, filled with the wisdom of the angels and the ancients. His gaze is one of vast invincible strength. He stands as immoveable as the mountains. There is peace and gentleness in his stance, but he cannot be either resisted or thwarted.

Druantia, the fir-tree goddess, presides over holy fire, the living sunlight. She fosters and directs the solar force. She will surround the unborn child from its conception to its birth with an infinitely tender expression and manifestation of this unconscionably powerful energy. See her as an all-loving, nurturing presence, reflecting the gentle might of Divine Mother.

Dana is a Welsh and Breton mother goddess. She is the spirit of Mother Earth, and her creative influences sing and sigh in rivers and streams. She urges all her children to give forth a perfect expression of their life forces. See this vital spirit breathing her life into the foetus and its uterine environment, bringing gifts of protection, stability and timely regulation.

Decoration Ideas

Whether you want to decorate a shortened scroll for display purposes or a full-length scroll for secretion, here are some ideas.

As a sign of protection, a bright silver equal-armed cross in a ring of golden light can be applied to the scroll.

For the angels, their protection is signified by these symbols:
- ⊕ *Afriel:* a ring of angels
- ⊕ *Brigid:* wheat ears, pearls, a lily and a rose
- ⊕ *Michael:* a winged disc and white rose petals
- ⊕ *Sandalphon:* a garland and an orb

For the Celtic deities, their signs are:
- ⊕ *Bran:* a raven, a leaf or two of sage, a crowned head and a golden pyramid set on its four-square base
- ⊕ *Druantia:* a miniature gilded pinecone
- ⊕ *Dana:* a small feather, to signify the holy breath or spirit

Colours you might select for this scroll include gold, green, fire colours and the soft duns of earth. (If you are inspired differently, it is always best to go with your own flow. An important point, however, is that any blessing scroll involving children should not include black).

Suitable crystals would be moss agate, amethyst, rose quartz, clear quartz and amber, corresponding respectively to the angelic spheres of nature forces, harmony, love and protection.

An appropriate aromatic oil would be rose, which corresponds to the angelic spheres of love, joy and purity.

Writing the Blessing

Before starting work on your blessing scroll, you will have assembled and blessed your materials, prayed to Brigid and Michael and intoned the Supplication to the Celtic Deities. Now intone the Rune of Intent:

'As I, (say your name), inscribe this scroll, I affirm that my act is holy, my heart pure, and my words vessels which I pray will be filled and blessed with the power of valiant Michael, Brightness of the Mountains, and Brigid of the Mantle, she who dwells in the golden heart of the sun. May Brigid and Michael bless and protect me and the work that I seek to achieve.'

Then write the Blessing:

'Afriel, Afriel, Afriel,
Glorious one,
Defender of the innocent,
Grand protector of the helpless,
Shield this child in your bright encircling.
Shield this child from all danger,
From all reversals, from all dismay.

No harm shall befall this descending soul
Beneath the white splendour
Of your three-cornered shield.

No hurt shall penetrate
The star-bright circuit
Of the victorious chief of safeguarding.
Afriel, Afriel, Afriel,
Tenderly Compassionate one,
Enfold this little soul
In your robes of fragrant light
In the innermost sanctuary
Which is your heart.

Joy of all joys,
Loveliness beyond comparing,
Be thou the cross of glory
To shield downward, upward, roundward,
To shield throughout life, and forever.'

(Note that in addition you will also write the Supplication to the Celtic Deities and a two-line prayer, both below in italic type.)

Intone the Prayer to Brigid and Michael:

'In the name of Brigid the Shining One,
In the name of the Great Chief,
I ask that my prayer for blessing be heard.
I ask that you purify my intention
And make my mind a mountain pool of clarity,
The fish in it leaping and silver
To summon the brightness of the blessing
From the hills of the angels.

May the Archangel Michael, and Brigid the Radiant
In whom dwells the presence of Divine Mother,
Of their benevolence,
Hear and grant my prayer.
By Brigid, by the Great Chief of the Angels, may it be so.'

Write the Supplication to the Celtic Deities:

'Bran, four-square strong,
Mighty peak of spiritual attainment,
Stand between this child
And all encroaching harm.

Druantia, burst of joyful sunlight
Flame of the heart of the sun,
Throw forth your rays as a bright halo,
Ringing this child around and around.

Dana, Beloved one,
Heart of the exalted Earth,
Let your Holy Breath
Infuse this child
With the Charm of Righteousness,
With the love of the Great Mother.'

For this blessing, instead of calling on Brigid, end the supplication with these words, to be pronounced firmly three times before being written on the scroll:

'The charm of God about thee, little one!
The arm of God above thee!'

Now you can decorate the scroll as you wish, before secreting the full-length scroll and displaying a shortened version of the scroll (if made) using the wording below.

SHORTENED BLESSING FOR THE DISPLAY SCROLL

'Afriel, Afriel, Afriel,
Tenderly Compassionate one,
Enfold this little soul
In the innermost sanctuary
Which is your heart.

Afriel, Afriel, Afriel,
Grand protector of the helpless,
Shield this child in your bright encircling.
Shield this child from all danger,
From all reversals, from all dismay.

No harm shall befall this descending soul;
No hurt shall penetrate
The star-bright circuit
Of the victorious chief of safeguarding.

Shield downward, upward, roundward,
Shield throughout life, and forever.'

12
BLESSING SCROLL
FOR THE BIRTH
OF A CHILD

The purpose of the Blessing Scroll for the Birth of a Child is to supplicate angelic protection for a mother as she gives birth to her child. The blessing's intention is also to bless her with strength and relief from pain during labour so that she can experience joy and a harmonius bonding with her baby during the process of giving birth.

The Angels

Ardousius, who presides over childbirth, brings to our higher senses a wonderfully subtle fragrance of the rose, of the divine feminine spirit. Her heart is like an enchanted cave secreting jewels or a sacred valley filled with rejoicing flowers. Throughout her being the radiation of inner fires moves as in musical cadences of starry brightness and poignant softness.

Feel her warmth surround you like a kindly embrace. Her eyes are radiant amber pools of nurturing love. Throughout her form sweeps a wave of turquoise blue, which tenderly relieves pain, and a golden swathe of vivid light, which sweeps away fear and danger. Rays of amethyst light and of rose light shine forth with a mystical luminosity from her brow. Her lips move in constant, compassionate blessing.

Behind her and around her, the birthing angels dance in perfect formation, creating beautiful geometric forms and adding their power and protection to hers. They are led by Armisael.

Above her stands Brigid, glorious golden one, both angel and goddess, woman of compassion and all-encompassing protection.

Adding his light to theirs, Archangel Michael stands as guardian of the spiritual sphere that they inhabit.

The Celtic Deities

⊕ *Arduinna*
⊕ *Coventina*
⊕ *Druantia*
⊕ *Epona*

Arduinna is a Celtic goddess of the forest and patroness of wild boar. Her name is intriguingly reminiscent of Ardousius, and in fact we see this protective angel of childbirth expressive of her full power in Arduinna.

A wonderful feminine expression of mighty strength and courage flows from Arduinna, which is there to serve the woman you wish to bless. Ardousius harmonizes the spate of this torrent by expressing it also as a self-replenishing flow of benevolence. This kindly flow is objectified by the easy and plentiful flow of breast milk that Ardousius fosters, while her twinned self, Arduinna, stands behind her as marshal of her power and holder of the secrets of the sacred forest, which concentrates solar force. Her colours are green and golden, the first denoting the heart and the last the sacred ring of everlasting light, which is the indwelling god force in creation.

Coventina is a goddess of sacred springs and healing wells. She is dressed in white, the perfect radiance of purity. Her magic is of the living waters, the waters of life. She grants safe childbirth and eases the violent force of the delivery. Her essence is kindly and loving, and she works with Ardousius to enable their combined angelic and exalted human influences (a stream from the heart of Goddess) to reach the birthing mother.

Druantia is the fir-tree goddess, protectress of mothers and of infants prior to, during and after birth. She is a deity of fire, and the fir (fire) tree whose essence she expresses is the holder of many mysteries, especially of the pineal gland or the third eye, which looks like a pinecone and opens and closes similarly. She is a coruscating tower of light, and she gives a steadfastness, an unassailable wisdom and a reassurance we can feel from great ancient trees if we attune sensitively to them.

Epona was the horse goddess of the ancient Celts. The white horse with which she is associated is linked to the concept and living presence of the dragon, the sacred serpent. The idea is that the fleet horse is the perfect manifesting vehicle for these wondrous feminine dragon powers to come into full expression on earth. The horse is the steed for their nobility. The seated woman is the serpent or the fiery soul and spirit essence, the horse beneath her not only the human body but also its manifold subtle vehicles dwelling within its chakra centres. The chakras are points on the body aligned with the spine and reaching to the head. They are associated with the ductless glands and are centres of reception for powers and influences flowing to us from the inner worlds, where physical and subtle reality interface and interchange their energies. They need to be cleansed occasionally by imagining an influx of celestial light which flows into and bathes each one. We can see how this supremely symbolic goddess is mistress of the forces that generate fertility, birthing and motherhood. Her colours are red, white and black.

Decoration Ideas

Whether you want to decorate a shortened scroll for display purposes or a full-length scroll for secretion, here are some ideas:

For the angels, their protection is signified by these symbols:

- ✢ *Ardousius:* jewels and a star emanating rays (symbolizing her fiery, love-centred protection)
- ✢ *Armisael:* the full moon
- ✢ *Brigid:* Brigid's cross, which is traditionally woven from grasses or reeds and takes the form of a saltire or St Andrew's Cross (X) with a square at its centre
- ✢ *Michael:* upraised sword with a white rose engraved on its hilt

For the Celtic deities, their signs are:

- ✢ *Arduinna:* a silver bow or quiver or small garland of leaves
- ✢ *Coventina:* a single piece of clear quartz
- ✢ *Druantia:* pine needles or a miniature pinecone
- ✢ *Epona:* a white horse, a dragon and a bird

Suitable crystals would be rose quartz, smithsonite, amber or moonstone. These crystals resonate with the respective angelic spheres of love, consolation, protection and regeneration.

An appropriate aromatic oil would be lavender, which is connected to the angelic spheres of protection, consolation and peace.

Writing the Blessing

Before starting work on your blessing scroll, you will have assembled and blessed your materials, prayed to Brigid and Michael and intoned the Supplication to the Celtic Deities. Now intone the Rune of Intent:

'As I, (say your name), inscribe this scroll, I affirm that my act is holy, my heart pure, and my words vessels which I pray will be filled and blessed with the power of valiant Michael, Brightness of the Mountains, and Brigid of the Mantle, she who dwells in the golden heart of the sun. May Brigid and Michael bless and protect me and the work that I seek to achieve.'

Then write the Blessing:

Ardousius, Ardousius, Ardousius,
Calm flame of purest beauty,
Armisael of the mercies,
Encircle (the name of the person to be blessed) in your
shining arms of strength.
Pour upon her the balm of your fragrant heart.
Hold her in the kindly fire of the gentle rose
and in the halls of the highest angels.
Hold her in the bright star of goodness
and in the rays of your compassion and blessing.

Encompass her in the brightest blessing of heaven,
and be thou to her a fortress of surpassing light.
Lend your power to her bringing forth,
Lend your protection to her delivery.'

(Note that in addition to the Blessing, you will also write the Supplication to the Celtic Deities and a one-line prayer to Brigid and Michael, both below in italic type.)

Intone the Prayer to Brigid and Michael:

'In the name of Brigid the Shining One,
In the name of the Great Chief,
I ask that my prayer for blessing be heard.
I ask that you purify my intention
And make my mind a mountain pool of clarity,
The fish in it leaping and silver
To summon the brightness of the blessing
From the hills of the angels.

May the Archangel Michael, and Brigid the Radiant
In whom dwells the presence of Divine Mother,
Of their benevolence,
Hear and grant my prayer.
By Brigid, by the Great Chief of the Angels, may it be so.'

Write the Supplication to the Celtic Deities:

'Arduinna, Mighty One,
Give your power of earth,
Of the charge and the victory,
In blessing to this birthing woman.

Coventina of the Living Springs,
Pure as the swan's breast,
Give the healing of your soothing waters
In blessing to this birthing woman.

Druantia, Star Fire of the forests,
Gracious one of the Holy Flame,
Give your perfect protection
In radiant blessing to this birthing woman.

Epona, Mistress of Air,
Bend your brow in blessing to this birthing woman.
Let the might of the powerful she-eagle
Sound forth in her cries,
And let her cries deliver her
From pain and travail
That she may bring forth
In safety, ease and joy.'

Finish the scroll by writing the words:

'By Brigid and by Michael, Great Chief of the Angels, may it be so.'

Now you can decorate the scroll as you wish, before secreting the full-length scroll and displaying a shortened version of the scroll (if made) using the wording opposite. Note, however, that the full blessing is of a suitable length to be accommodated by the display scroll.

SHORTENED BLESSING FOR THE DISPLAY SCROLL

'Ardousius, Ardousius, Ardousius,
Calm flame of purest beauty,
Armisael of the mercies,
Encircle (the name of the person to be blessed) in your
shining arms of strength.
Pour upon her the balm of your fragrant heart.
Hold her in the kindly fire of the gentle rose
and in the halls of the highest angels.
Hold her in the bright star of goodness
and in the rays of your compassion and blessing.
Encompass her in the brightest blessing of heaven,
and be thou to her a fortress of surpassing light.
Lend your power to her bringing forth,
Lend your protection to her delivery.'

13
BLESSING SCROLL
FOR A
NEWBORN CHILD

Of all the blessing scrolls, perhaps this one lends itself most to beautiful and poignant decoration. If you are making a display scroll, it will be beneficial to convey something of tenderness and sweetness by its construction, in keeping with the baby's aura and the angels' nurturing of it. At birth, the aura is uniquely clear and pure and naturally contains angelic frequencies.

The Angels

Archangel Shekinah and Archangel Michael stand as mighty pillars of light to give their blessing and shielding to the child you bring before them. Mikhar and Raphael, presiding angels over the heavenly baptismal waters, wait upon these supreme two, ready to do their bidding in this momentous act of blessing.

Shekinah shines forth with a brilliance that is brighter than all the stars of the universe, yet she does not dazzle or cause human eyes to flinch from her. Instead, she warmly invites you to step onto a silver road that leads straight to her heart. The silver from which this road is composed causes joy to stir and leap in our own hearts. It is called 'the loveliest of all that is lovely', and is the perfect harmonization of gold and silver: the supreme expression of Shekinah and Michael as a single seamless being.

A young woman who bore the Shekinah energies was spoken of as the most beautiful woman ever to have lived. She was known as Mary Hynes, a nineteenth-century Irish girl. Children, women and men fell silent before her, in awe and reverence for her loveliness and the mystical potency of her presence.

Her hair, renowned for its enchantment of beauty and the way it seemed to throw off effulgence, was the colour of the path to Shekinah's heart – a wondrous combination of silver and gold.

The pure and radiant soul of Mary Hynes had, with marvellous spiritual skill, blended with Shekinah's essence as a poignant reminder that within each member of humanity lies enshrined the potential to rise even higher than the greatest angels. We can draw inspiration from Mary Hynes and take the road direct to Shekinah's heart in all confidence that we, too, can enter the temple of her heart and become consummate with the limitless love, healing, protection and benevolence that enfold us there.

Within the heart of Shekinah we can stand in the innermost presence of this supreme one, and also enter into communion with Archangel Michael, magnificently radiant. Archangel Michael was the original slayer of the dragon (St George is a human expression of his energies), and his awe-inspiring authority sweeps away every shadow and encroachment. The dragon he felled was the dragon of the lower expression of life – all that corrupts, distorts and darkens perception. Michael himself is often portrayed as a serpent: the golden serpent of supernal consciousness, expressing God. His sacred task is to prevent the lower earthly saurian from swallowing us in its coils and causing us to forget our divine serpent essence.

Shekinah and Michael nurture all that is noble in the human soul. Their arms are filled with an abundance of blessings and gifts for every newborn child who is brought into their presence. Bathe in this ineffable presence. See the child you wish to bless being received into it. The grand and sweet encirclement of Shekinah and Michael will catch you up into bliss.

The Celtic Deities
⊕ Brigid
⊕ Taliesin

Brigid was the supreme goddess of the Celts. She was universally beloved, the Druids in particular regarding her as a being of unsurpassed purity and light. She is associated with Shekinah in that this angelic being is an expression of Brigid's own angelic qualities, for Brigid encompasses all worlds. She was called the 'foster mother' of Christ, and indeed she was, because she fostered Christ consciousness in the West long, long before it arrived from the East in truncated form as a religion. She has three aspects: Brigid of the Radiant Flame (her spirit), Brigid of the

Divine Forges – the Smithwoman who forges creation from the Radiant Flame (her soul) – and Brigid the Crone, the Ancient of Days, whose mysterious being enshrines the wisdom of the Earth and the manifesting physical world of matter (her body). She was known to her people as the Woman of Compassion, the Woman of Healing, the Woman of Inspiration, the Woman of Miracles.

Essentially she is the Bride, the feminine aspect of the great Christ being in the heavens, the Daughter of God. Her capacity for blessings and precious gifts of the soul can only be described as bounteous.

Taliesin was said to be the magical son of Cerridwen, a potent goddess whose enchanted cauldron was the source of her vast power. She had taken on a servant, Gwion, an ugly, misshapen youth of stunted growth who served her well. He was instructed to attend her wondrous Cauldron of Inspiration, but never to taste of its contents.

One day, Gwion scalded his finger by accident in the contents of the cauldron, and sucked it to ease the pain. He was instantly transformed into a magician. Cerridwen, on returning, challenged him for his disobedience and set off in pursuit of him. A shapeshifting contest ensued, which Cerridwen won by changing herself into a black hen and eating Gwion after he had taken the form of a grain of wheat.

Nine months later, Cerridwen gave birth to beautiful Taliesin, Radiant Brow, prophet, philosopher, spiritual teacher and peerless bard, who was drawn like Moses from the water in a little rustic vessel. (These special circumstances of his discovery as an infant identify Taliesin, in common with several gods before him, as a deity.) He appeared on Earth in human form shortly after the fall of Arthur, and his mysterious poetry, with its cadences of beauty, lives on today. Taliesin came forth from the Goddess as the perfect son of light, transformed by his journey through the underworld of her challenges and transfigured by his final sacrifice. Every gift was given to him, and he in turn will offer every gift and blessing to souls new born into the challenges of their own light.

Decoration Ideas

Whether you want to decorate a shortened scroll for display purposes or a full-length scroll for secretion, here are some ideas:

Seed pearls are symbolic of newborns, as are hand-made lace, rosebuds and acorns. Pieces of eggshell, washed in pastel colours, also signify a birth. Mother-of-pearl provides beautiful, significant decoration for a new life, even if you can find only buttons! Shoes are indicative of setting out on life's path, and a pair of tiny shoes, sprayed with silver, show that the soul is silver-shod. Silver shoes reflect the light of heaven as the soul treads its earthly path. Silver and golden coins are emblematic of abundance, as are cornucopias filled with fruit and flowers.

Colours for this scroll should be delicate pastel shades – nothing dark, heavy or vivid is suitable.

For the angels, their protection is signified by these symbols:
- ⊕ *Shekinah:* an ascending golden bird
- ⊕ *Michael:* white rose petals and a golden, crowned serpent
- ⊕ *Raphael:* a caduceus (two opposing serpents twining around a staff)
- ⊕ *Mikhar:* a dove and a mountain spring

For the Celtic deities, their signs are:
- ⊕ *Brigid:* pearls, dandelion petals, rowan and hawthorn berries and the sacred spiral
- ⊕ *Taliesin:* the Celtic harp, a star in a pool, a leaping salmon, a boat, a swan and swansdown

THE ANGEL BLESSING SCROLLS: BLESSING 13

Suitable crystals would be clear quartz and rose quartz, correlating to the angelic spheres of purity and protection, and love, joy and wisdom.

An appropriate aromatic oil would be rose, corresponding to the angelic spheres of love, joy and purity. Rose fragrance is in itself a powerful healer and enshrines its own blessing.

Writing the Blessing

Before starting work on your blessing scroll, you will have assembled and blessed your materials, prayed to Brigid and Michael and intoned the Supplication to the Celtic Deities. Now intone the Rune of Intent:

'As I, (say your name), inscribe this scroll, I affirm that my act is holy, my heart pure, and my words vessels which I pray will be filled and blessed with the power of valiant Michael, Brightness of the Mountains, and Brigid of the Mantle, she who dwells in the golden heart of the sun. May Brigid and Michael bless and protect me and the work that I seek to achieve.'

Before writing the Blessing, call on the four angels Shekinah, Michael, Raphael and Mikhar, and the deities Brigid and Taliesin, to be present and to focus their blessings on the child while it is given the ancient baptismal blessing in spiritual waters. Chant the names of the angels and deities, and supplicate their presence by name. (Please note that this blessing is lengthy, in accordance with the traditional art of baptismal blessing where gifts for the child are summoned from heaven and delivered by the angels, so unless you decide on a shortened version, the scroll will extend to an appreciable length.) Imagining that these six bright ones stand in a circle around you and the child, facilitating the baptismal blessing, write these words:

'I bathe thy palms
In showers of wine,
In the lustral fire,
In the seven elements,
In the juice of the rasps,
In the milk of honey,
And I place the nine pure choice graces
In thy fair fond face.

A wavelet for thy form,
A wavelet for thy voice,
A wavelet for thy sweet speech,
A wavelet for thy luck,
A wavelet for thy good,
A wavelet for thy health,

A wavelet for thy throat,
A wavelet for thy pluck,
A wavelet for thy graciousness;
Nine waves for thy graciousness.

Grace of form,
Grace of fortune,
Grace of voice,
Grace of the Son of Peace be ever thine,
Grace of the image of God be thine.

Grace of men,
Grace of women,
Grace of lover,
Grace of sons and daughters be thine.

Grace of eating,
Grace of drinking,
Grace of music,
Grace of guidance,
Grace of sea and land be thine.
Grace of rest,
Grace of journeying,
Grace of silence,
Grace of dreaming be thine.

Grace of the wild duck,
Grace of the swan of the fountain,
Grace of every kindliness and comfort;
Enduring grace by day and by night be thine.

Grace of the love of the skies be thine,
Grace of the love of the stars be thine,
Grace of the love of the moon be thine,
Grace of the love of the sun be thine,
Grace of the love of the crown of heaven be thine.

Thou art the joy of all joyous things,
Thou art the light of the beam of the sun.

The lovely likeness of God
Is in thy pure face,
The loveliest likeness
That was upon earth.'

(Note that in addition to the Blessing itself, you will also write the Supplication to the Celtic Deities and a one-line prayer to Brigid and Michael, both overleaf in italic type.)

Intone the Prayer to Brigid and Michael:

'In the name of Brigid the Shining One,
In the name of the Great Chief,
I ask that my prayer for blessing be heard.

I ask that you purify my intention
And make my mind a mountain pool of clarity,
The fish in it leaping and silver
To summon the brightness of the blessing
From the hills of the angels.

May the Archangel Michael, and Brigid the Radiant
In whom dwells the presence of Divine Mother,
Of their benevolence,
Hear and grant my prayer.
By Brigid, by the Great Chief of the Angels, may it be so.'

Write the Supplication to the Celtic Deities:

'Brigid of the graces,
Brigid of whole-souled loveliness,
Give to this child
The nine pure choice graces.

Taliesin, Radiant Brow,
Encircle this child
With your ring of bright gifts.
Be to this child
The surpassing star of guidance.'

Finish the scroll by writing the words:

'By Brigid and by Michael, Great Chief of the Angels, may it be so.'

Now you can decorate the scroll as you wish, before secreting the full-length scroll and displaying a shortened version of the scroll (if made) using the wording opposite.

SHORTEΠED BLESSIΠG FOR THE DISPLAY SCROLL

'I bathe thy palms
In the lustral fire,
In the seven elements,
In the milk of honey,
And I place the nine pure choice graces
In thy fair fond face.

Grace of form,
Grace of fortune,
Grace of voice,
Grace of the Son of Peace be ever thine,
Grace of the image of God be thine.
Grace of men,
Grace of women,
Grace of lover,
Grace of sons and daughters be thine.

Thou art the joy of all joyous things,
Thou art the light of the beam of the sun.'

14
BLESSING SCROLL
FOR
FERTILITY

The angels of fertility may be called on via this blessing scroll, either to facilitate a general supplication for a person's fertility or to intervene where there is a problem. It is important for the recipient of the scroll to create time and space each day for inner listening, as the angels may need to send messages concerning diet, breathing, posture and even which doctor to consult.

The Angels

It is helpful to think of the angels of fertility as surrounding and emerging from a cauldron or a universal cup, which is the Holy Grail. We need to construct this cauldron in our hearts and minds as we create this blessing scroll, as though we are brewing up a powerful and hallowed elixir – a drop of the Grail essence that we can imbibe and send as a blessing to the recipient of the scroll.

Angels of the moon and angels of Venus are among those concerned with fertility. The angels of the moon, softly shining, move in mysterious, gently muted configurations until they reach a crescendo of magnetism and brilliance, which we might associate with the full moon. They then seem to take an in-breath and recede, as if we must heighten our spiritual senses to perceive them until they return on the following out-breath.

The angels of Venus are jubilant and of an intensity of beauty that opens the heart in wonder. They are of a transcendental purity, profoundly white, although they also manifest in colours. The heavenly pink of the interior of a conch shell and the rose of the first blush of sunrise are their colours, as well as hues of blue and green. For purposes of fertility, it is helpful to think of an emerald jewel and to bathe in its deep essence of sanctified radiant green. The angels of the moon and of Venus will draw close to bless your intention.

Gabriel, Samandiriel, Anael, Anahita and Barbelo also govern and bless fertility. Gabriel brings the mystical silver of the moon and its power of fertility in her wings; Samandiriel, bright angel over imagination, also conveys the magical forces of the silver cosmic mirror, principle of conception and creation, in blessing; Anael, angel of the mystery at the heart of the rose and called the angel of the star of love, fosters the benediction of Venus and her angels; Anahita is the angel of fruitfulness; Barbelo reignites our everlasting youth – its fiery ideals and forces of highest potency.

Shekinah and Zadkiel will bless endeavours to conceive. They convey a golden encompassment of sublime protection and favourable circumstances.

Call finally on archangel Raphael, who brings healing and resolution to all human difficulties.

The Celtic Deities

⊕ *Brigid*
⊕ *Merlin*
⊕ *Modron*
⊕ *Grainne*
⊕ *Boann*
⊕ *Dana*
⊕ *Aine*
⊕ *Cerridwen*
⊕ *Columba*
⊕ *Morgan*

Brigid, the Bride, is associated with the magical tides of the moon and Venus, and is the goddess of the Divine Forges, where creation is wrought in supernal fire. She was known in the Scottish Western Isles as the Blessed Woman of Compassion. She will grant her aid in fertility supplications.

Merlin, deity of the Secret of the Tree, blesses the mystery of human bloodlines (the 'family tree'), and may be called upon to add his magic to the 'cauldron' of blessing you are creating.

Modron is the Welsh Mother Goddess of ancient times and presides over the harvest, the gentle release of the soul as it is birthed into the spiritual spheres at the time of its ascension, and the healing waters that bring renewal, mercy and fertility.

Grainne ('Grawn-ya') is an Irish goddess of the sun. Rather than marry the hero Fionn in his declining years, Grainne refused his courtship and ran away with the youthful Diarmuid, who was Fionn's most beloved friend. The terrible and haunting sorrow she caused poor Fionn taught her to have compassion on age and the ageing process and to respect its gifts and virtues. Although her great task was to carry fertility to the Earth each spring, Grainne was given special powers of mediation between youth and age, bringing one to the other and merging their aspirations, ideals and qualities. She can help especially in cases where age is a factor affecting fertility.

Boann is an Irish mother goddess of fertility. She presides over the living waters within the womb, and over Earth's flowing waters and their fertilizing power. She will work with Modron to bless a woman's desire to conceive a child.

Dana, a Welsh and Breton mother goddess, is the spirit of Mother Earth, and her creative influences sing and sigh in rivers and streams. She urges all her children to give forth a perfect expression of their life forces. See this vital spirit breathing her life into the womb or the loins of the would-be mother and father as you craft your scroll. Dana adds her forces to those of Boann and Modron, and is helpful in cases where the fertility problem is on the masculine side.

Aine ('Aw-ne'), Irish goddess of the sun and moon and bountiful Lady of the Harvest, smiles on petitions for fertility. She was known as a fairy princess who sometimes took the form of a swan. Her swan-maiden identity reveals her as a healer, as there are many stories of enchanted swans that bring miraculous healing to humans in the Celtic pantheon. She helps to attune our bodies to their natural rhythms and our souls to the grand cycles of nature. She will 'turn the wheel' and bring renewed hope and potential to difficult circumstances. She connects us to the laughing vivacity of the fairies, who in their own right can bring fulfillment to our wish for a child.

Cerridwen is the Goddess of the Cauldron, which is a cosm cally mystical device akin to the Holy Grail. She presides as imaginally construct our cauldron and set it boiling with ange and deific presences. She will bestow co-ordination of this gr magical act of supplication for blessing, and will lend her pow of inspiration to the process from start to finish. Be especia mindful of respect when you address Cerridwen! She does n suffer fools gladly, nor those who fail to respect her cauldron.

Columba, beneficent and compassionate, who overcame own inner blockages and difficulties to lead a saintly life, w bless your request for fertility with an outcome that encompass his mercy.

Morgan is the supreme mistress of the Grail, and is its e ence. Make your final supplication to her so that Brigid a Morgan are the alpha and omega of your work with the Cel deities for this scroll.

Decoration Ideas

Whether you want to decorate a shortened scroll for display p poses or a full-length scroll for secretion, here are some ideas inspire you.

There are many symbols for fertility, as teeming as the c cept itself. Some of the most powerful include:

- ✠ *The 'three Marys':* Mary, the mother of Jesus, Mary Jacob, the mother of Mary Magdalene, and Mary Magdalene herself. Traditionally, they are portrayed in a circle, with a mermaid at its centre point. This design in itself is an ancient invocation for fertility.
- ✠ *eight dancing legs* moving sunwise or clockwise in a ring, which creates the positive, Buddhist swastika – a powerful symbol of the life forces

⊕ *a shoe* – an ornamental miniature shoe or a baby's shoe

⊕ *flowers*, such as white lilies and apple blossom

⊕ *fruits*, such as vines bearing grapes

⊕ *seeds*, such as apple pips, or the contents from the pod of any plant after it has flowered

⊕ *the corn dolly, the fig tree and the cornucopia*, which symbolize fruitfulness and bringing forth

⊕ *horseshoes* (representing the sacred mare of the Earth's fertility)

⊕ *bird houses* (representing the dwelling place of the great mother goddess)

⊕ *the figure 8*, denoting life's continuous flow, either upright or on its side, or represented in both modes.

For the angels, their protection is signified by these symbols:

⊕ *The angels of the moon:* a silver mirror, the crescent, half and full moon

⊕ *The angels of Venus:* an emerald jewel

⊕ *Gabriel:* a chaplet of roses

⊕ *Samandiriel:* an egg with the golden ring of infinity secreted within it

⊕ *Anael:* a full-blown red rose with golden sepals

⊕ *Anahita:* an apple tree in its late-summer fruitfulness

⊕ *Barbelo:* a cloak of radiant fire; a celestial spring (in the heavens, with a flow of gold downwards to Earth)

⊕ *Shekinah:* an ascending golden bird; enfolding angel wings

⊕ *Zadkiel:* a violet flame

⊕ *Raphael:* the caduceus

For the Celtic deities, their signs are:

⊕ *Brigid:* pearls, rowan berries and a plume of flames

⊕ *Merlin:* a leaf, bark, an acorn and a wren

- *Modron:* a cornucopia, grains of corn, a butterfly and a fountain
- *Grainne:* an evergreen leaf and everlasting flowers
- *Boann:* a silver orb reflecting a fountain
- *Dana:* a lily, a dewdrop, a star and the figure 8, either upright or horizontal
- *Aine:* a dragonfly, a wheel of the seasons and a swan wearing a golden chain around its neck and falling on its breast
- *Cerridwen:* a cauldron reflecting stars
- *Columba:* a dove brooding eggs
- *Morgan:* a golden jewelled cup

Suitable crystals would be moonstone, zoisite, alexandrite (for the male reproductive organs) and rhodonite, which bless and stimulate fertility; they correspond to the angelic spheres of new beginnings, new patterning and encodings, flowering and fruitfulness.

Appropriate aromatic oils would be lavender, sandalwood and rose, which correspond to the angelic spheres of serenity, stillness and radiant peace. Sandalwood plays a balancing and connecting role in linking our awareness to these spheres.

Writing the Blessing

Before starting work on your blessing scroll, you will have assembled and blessed your materials, prayed to Brigid and Michael and intoned the Supplication to the Celtic Deities. Now intone the Rune of Intent:

'As I, (say your name), inscribe this scroll, I affirm that my act is holy, my heart pure, and my words vessels which I pray will be filled and blessed with the power of valiant Michael, Brightness of the Mountains, and Brigid of the Mantle, she who dwells in the golden heart of the sun. May Brigid and Michael bless and protect me and the work that I seek to achieve.'

Then write the Blessing (inserting the name of the recipient or object of the scroll where appropriate):

'I invoke the cauldron of potency
The Blessed Cup, the Cup of Mary,
Mary, lovely of joys,
Mary, lovely of sorrows.

I invoke the cauldron of divine fruitfulness.
Around its brimming rim
Are Samandiriel, measurelessly bright,
Anahita of the flowering orchards,
Barbelo of fragrant abundance and the hope of heaven.
I invoke the cauldron of a confluence of blessings,
Blessings of the day spring on high.
Around its brimming rim
Are Gabriel, gift of the moon,
Anael, angel of the morning star,
Shekinah of the shining mercies,
Zadkiel, holy angel of the gladsome Grail.

And to you, (insert name),
Beloved of the angels,
On you may their blessings descend,
As a bright flame of holiest fire,
As the spark that will grant you the child you long for.

Power of raven be yours,
Power of eagle be yours,
Power of the Fiann.

Power of stars be yours,
Power of moon be yours,
Power of sun.

Power of prayers be yours,
Power of planets,
Power of saints.

Power of wind be yours,
Power of rain,
Power of dew.

Power of sea be yours,
Power of land be yours,
Power of heaven.

Goodness of sea be yours,
Goodness of earth be yours,
Goodness of heaven.

Power of angels be given to you
In blessing to fulfill your prayer.

In presence of the holy angels of heaven,
In presence of Raphael of beauteous form,
If truly a blessing,
May this blessing be given to you, (insert name),
Beseecher of angels,
Beloved and protected of angels.'

(Note that in addition to the Blessing, you will also write the Supplication to the Celtic Deities and a one-line prayer to Brigid, both below in italic type.)

Intone the Prayer to Brigid and Michael:

'In the name of Brigid the Shining One,
In the name of the Great Chief,
I ask that my prayer for blessing be heard.
I ask that you purify my intention
And make my mind a mountain pool of clarity,
The fish in it leaping and silver
To summon the brightness of the blessing
From the hills of the angels.

May the Archangel Michael, and Brigid the Radiant
In whom dwells the presence of Divine Mother,
Of their benevolence,
Hear and grant my prayer.
By Brigid, by the Great Chief of the Angels, may it be so.'

Write the Supplication to the Celtic Deities (shortened to just a
sentence for each deity, as there are so many of them):

*'Brigid of Light, Mistress of the Divine Forges,
bestow your spark of holy fire on this enterprise.*

*Merlin, Keeper of the Secret of the Tree,
add your beneficent magic to this sacred cauldron.*

*Modron, of your bounty, and your power of blessed release
from all yearning and striving, add your potency to this blessing.*

*Grainne of the open heart, who shines youth and its potencies
into the grace and garnering of age and makes both golden,
bestow your miracle of mercy on this work.*

Boann, kindly mother, goddess of the running wave,
of the flowing waters of earth and the living waters within,
grant your fertilizing power to this blessing.

Dana of the Powers, goodly goddess of the springing seed,
direct your beautiful harmonized life-forces into this cauldron
of blessing.

Aine, Lady of the Harvest, swan-maiden and princess of the fays,
summon the fairy blessing with its dancing lights to enhance this work,
and put your word of power into this sacred cauldron.

Cerridwen, Mistress of the Cauldron of Inspiration,
breathe your goodly influences into the living waters of this caul-
dron of blessing and orientate its forces towards a fruitful outcome.

Columba, compassionate heart, of your mercy,
bless the prayer of this woman [or man] for fertility with fulfillment.

Morgan, Lady of the Holy Grail, sacred drop of the divine essence,
hear this prayer for fertility and bless it with joyful realization.'

Finish the scroll by writing the words:

'*By Brigid and by Michael, Great Chief of the Angels, may it be so.*'

Now you can decorate the scroll as you wish, before secreting the
full-length scroll and displaying a shortened version of the scroll
(if made) using the wording opposite.

SHORTENED BLESSING FOR
THE DISPLAY SCROLL

'I invoke the cauldron of potency.
The Blessed Cup, the Cup of Mary,

I invoke the cauldron of divine fruitfulness.
Around its brimming rim
Are Samandiriel, measurelessly bright,
Anahita of the flowering orchards,
Barbelo of fragrant abundance and the hope of heaven.

I invoke the cauldron of a confluence of blessings.
Around its brimming rim
Are Gabriel, gift of the moon,
Anael, angel of the morning star,
Shekinah of the shining mercies,
Zadkiel, holy angel of the gladsome Grail.

And to you, (insert name),
Beloved of the angels,
On you may their blessings descend,
As a bright flame of holiest fire,
As the spark that will grant you the child you long for.'

15

BLESSING SCROLL
FOR
HEALING

Although this scroll invokes a blessing for healing people, it can also be used in order to supplicate healing for an animal, a body of water, a wood or a meadow, a garden or a tree or plant, or even a room or a building. You can make use of it in creative ways, such as in the case of a fraught situation, a negative tendency or some pattern of consistent bad luck.

The Angels

The great archangel of healing is Raphael, whose mystery manifests in equal measure through feminine and masculine aspects. All healing flows forth from Raphael. His key word is 'consolamentum', the title of a secret ceremony administered by the Cathars of medieval France, by means of which their priests dispensed spiritual wholeness and an unfettered vision of the higher worlds. This word vibrates throughout his being. In itself it can soothe and restore, and summon the magic of healing to the ailing, fragmented soul.

Raphael's form is mighty, as tall as a cathedral. His eyes shine with loving compassion, emitting a great light, and yet they are as mellow and gentle and deep as the glow of ancient and mysterious gold. His lips utter rhythmic healing chants, beautiful in their vibration, becoming from time to time a great burst of exquisite song, which pierces the listening soul with an irresistible tide of love as renewal, as reawakening, as revivification. Hear his soft chanting and his burst of song through which the cadence of the word 'consolamentum' beats like a spirit drum.

There is the fragrance of cleansing joy in the robes of Raphael, and golden healing in his wings. Let those golden wings of light enfold you in their great arcs of sweeping spiritual force, and know yourself as perfect in light, perfect, perfect within the sunlight of his healing embrace.

Now see his vast host of healing angels as they come in countless choirs to the golden-winged feet of their master, ready to receive his blessing and the touch of his radiant hands, which bestow the gift of spiritual life-forces from the ineffable and cosmic reservoir that is his/her very being.

Some come on Raphael's own golden ray, bright and deep in hue, some gently glowing as with the marigold light of a summer evening sun, some with the light of the early morning rays.

Some come in on a single colour ray, all blending in an assembled mystery of soft rose, or glowing emerald-green or sweet heavenly blue.

Some sweep in like a tide, arrayed in iridescent rainbow colours, subtle, shimmering and beautiful, as though their hues shone through the purest crystal.

Some bear a most holy pearlescent light, which is wonderful to see: the pearly light of noble unicorns from the high places of the soul, and of precious stones from a sublime sea that beats on the shores of Paradise.

A great host of the healing angels are dressed in simple garments of the purest white, an unearthly whiteness that is so vast and deep that it is the heart of peace itself, making earthly whiteness seem almost dark in comparison. Yet you may note how soft and gentle to the eye is the whiteness of these sacred garments, a whiteness that does not dazzle, as if pushing away, but rather tenderly enfolds you in its magical light.

Draw near to Archangel Raphael and his great host of angels. Absorb the consciousness and the forces that their aura emanates. Whether you are making this blessing scroll for yourself or for a friend, you will need to be a strong and sure conduit for the healing angels.

If the scroll is intended as a general blessing for good health, or if the healing you require is emotional rather than physical, it will not be necessary to call on other angels. However, if you, or the person for whom the scroll is intended, suffer from a serious illness, include the angel Malachi in your meditations and add his name to your written blessing. Malachi stands in state in the sphere of finalities. He rules the beginning and the end point in the creational scheme, which is essentially the same. If it is lawful, he will bring closure and demise to the cycle of suffering you wish to end.

In cases of serious illness, call also, through the written and the spoken word, on the angel Sabriel, chief of the order of Tarshishim, the 'brilliant ones' associated with the virtues. Sabriel, shining with the light of a thousand stars, overcomes and banishes, returning the soul to its pristine state of ease, peace and grace.

The Celtic Deities

✛ *Brigid*
✛ *Columba*
✛ *Arianrhod*

Brigid dispenses healing and wholeness to those who make heart-contact with her. Known as the Triple Goddess, she gently enfolds our three aspects (mind, body, spirit) in her pure and perfect light. Some people experience this as being taken into the folds of her radiant garments. The Scottish islanders understood Brigid's encompassing as a conducting inwards into her 'pure sheepfolds', speaking of her with unsurpassed love and reverence as 'Brigid of the Mantle' (see under Blessing Scroll for a Newborn Child).

Columba was known for his compassion and personal concern for the Scottish communities with whom he worked. He was gifted with the healing power of both the angels and the Christ-essence, and would often hurry away from meals and gatherings to pray for some remote suffering soul whom he sensed was reaching out to him for help (see under Blessing Scroll for a New Home, page 112).

Arianrhod is the Welsh Goddess of the full moon, of time and destiny. She is one of the famed 'spinning goddesses' who produce silver threads from their own soul essence with which to weave the destinies of human souls. We see in this 'spinning' signature a reference to the power that sustains worlds and universes. Arianrhod was mistress of a glass tower or spiral castle whose configurations are those of the soul. She is keeper of our spinning chakras, which, when purified and fully activated, do indeed create a crystal tower or spiralling castle known as the 'soul shrine'. It protects us and frees us when it is perfected, because from then on no path or resonance is closed to us. While we are occupied with the task of bringing it to perfection, however, it can sometimes seem like a prison filled with taskmaster wardens! Arianrhod's mystical castle was traditionally the place where poets and musicians brought their art to perfection, because, of course, the calibre of the soul must always be that of master poet and musician.

Arianrhod purges and cleanses, and restores balance, harmony and right resonance to our chakras. If we will commune in sincerity with her, she will protect our health and cast out disease.

Decoration Ideas

Whether you want to decorate a shortened scroll for display purposes or a full-length scroll for secretion, here are some ideas to inspire you.

There are innumerable symbols for healing and good health. Choose those to which you feel most drawn, yet also include the cross of light within the circle of light, as it is perhaps the most powerful, together with the six-pointed star. This is formed from two equilateral triangles, one pointing upwards and the other downwards. It is important to note, however, that this mystical star does not contain the inner divisions of the Star of David. It is a symbol of wholeness.

The unicorn is a healing symbol, as is the dragon. The caduceus (a staff around which coil two opposing snakes from foot to tip) is the supreme healing emblem of our Western civilization, formally adopted by orthodox medical establishments since the era of ancient Greece, although its origins lie in a much earlier Mesopotamian tradition. It is the sign and symbol of Archangel Raphael.

The Tree of Life, the pine tree, the olive tree, the rowan, the rose and the apple are all-powerful healing symbols. The true swastika (in contradistinction to the abomination that the Nazis used), which portrays eight dancing legs moving sunwise or clockwise in a circle, is a holistic symbol, as is the budding rod, the ring and the rainbow. The Egyptian ankh, the pyramid and the cross are all beautiful healing seals, as is the tai-chi-tu (the Chinese symbol denoting the yin and yang forces).

For the angel, his protection is signified by this symbol:
⊕ *Raphael*: caduceus

For the Celtic deities, their signs are:
⊕ *Brigid*: dandelion
⊕ *Columba*: trefoil
⊕ *Arianrhod:* silver thread and clear quartz crystal

Suitable crystals would be any of the numerous crystals that have healing properties. Bloodstone, emerald, clear and rose quartz are comforting and familiar healing energies to work with. They can be augmented with celestite and angelite. All of these crystals correspond to the angelic realms of healing.

Appropriate aromatic oils would be rosemary, lavender, rose, frankincense and bergamot, which correspond to the angelic spheres of protection and healing.

Writing the Blessing

Before starting work on your blessing scroll, you will have assembled and blessed your materials, prayed to Brigid and

Michael and intoned the Supplication to the Celtic Deities. Now intone the Rune of Intent:

'As I, (say your name), inscribe this scroll, I affirm that my act is holy, my heart pure, and my words vessels which I pray will be filled and blessed with the power of valiant Michael, Brightness of the Mountains, and Brigid of the Mantle, she who dwells in the golden heart of the sun. May Brigid and Michael bless and protect me and the work that I seek to achieve.'

Then write the Blessing, personalizing it by beginning it with the name of the person to whom it is addressed:

'The shield of Michael is over you,
King of the bright angels;
He is shielding and encircling you
From your summit to your sole.

Raphael, glorious one,
Coming to you in raiment of rainbows,
Coming to you on rays of angels
Arrayed in rainbow garments
Fresher than the first rays of the morning.

(Insert recipient's name)
You are the love of the God of Life,
You are the love of the Son of Light,
You are the love of Mary of the Purities,
You are the love of Brigid the Beauteous,
You are the love of Holy Spirit,
You are the love of each living creature.
Hail, Raphael of all healing!

Power of heaven and power of God is yours!
By the power of the highest love,
Make and preserve this beloved one whole!
Peace and light be,
Peace of love be,
Peace of healing be,
Peace of wholeness forever be yours,
Peace of wholeness forever be yours,
You, (insert name), who are beloved of angels and of God.'

(Note that in addition to the Blessing, you will also write the Supplication to the Celtic Deities and a one-line prayer to Brigid and Michael, both below in italic type.)

Intone the Prayer to Brigid and Michael:

'In the name of Brigid the Shining One,
In the name of the Great Chief,
I ask that my prayer for blessing be heard.
I ask that you purify my intention
And make my mind a mountain pool of clarity,
The fish in it leaping and silver
To summon the brightness of the blessing
From the hills of the angels.

May the Archangel Michael, and Brigid the Radiant
In whom dwells the presence of Divine Mother,
Of their benevolence,
Hear and grant my prayer.
By Brigid, by the Great Chief of the Angels, may it be so.'

Write the Supplication to the Celtic Deities:

'Encircling of Brigid the beloved be yours;
At night her fair starlight laves you in milk of wholeness;
At dawn of day you are in the healing heart of her lustral fires.
Kindly Columba guide you
To the heart of all healing,
To the shrine of the seven joys;
Kindly Columba protect and bless you
With the seven joys of wholeness.

Arianrhod of the silver hand,
Bless the seven lamps of this beloved soul;
Light them with the sublime silver of the stars;
Cast out from them all that is not gracious;
Fulfil in them the light of the Lightener of the Stars.'

Finish the scroll by writing the words:

'By Brigid and by Michael, Great Chief of the Angels, may it be so.'

Now you can decorate the scroll as you wish, before secreting the full-length scroll and displaying a shortened version of the scroll (if made) using the wording opposite.

SHORTENED BLESSING FOR
THE DISPLAY SCROLL

'(Insert recipient's name)
The shield of Michael is over you,
King of the bright angels;
He is shielding and encircling you
From your summit to your sole.

Raphael, glorious one,
Coming to you in raiment of rainbows,
Coming to you on rays of angels
Arrayed in rainbow garments
Fresher than the first rays of the morning.

Hail, Raphael of all healing!
Power of heaven and power of God is yours!
By the power of the highest love,
Make and preserve this beloved one whole!

Peace of wholeness forever be yours,
Peace of wholeness forever be yours,
You, (insert name), who are beloved of angels and of God.'

16
BLESSING SCROLL
FOR PROTECTING A MEMBER OF THE ARMED FORCES

If someone you know is due to be sent on a military mission, you can create a blessing scroll specifically for their protection. Just replace the first-person wording of the Blessing and Supplication of the Celtic Deities with the name of the person for whom it is intended. The Ring of Angels encourages the recipient of the blessing never to cause death or injury unless it is unavoidable.

The Angels

Archangel Michael is the first angel to greet our perception in this holy ring. Golden-haired, armed with light, astride a white horse, his place is beside Shekinah, Lady of the Golden Shielding, whose glory is irresistible. Zazriel towers alongside this supreme pair, angelic prince of the divine strength, might and power. The immense dynamism of Ribkiel is the next link in the ring, he who divinely guides through danger. To complete the protective circle, we call on the holy angels Alimon, Reivtip and Tafthi, who together protect against ambush, gunshot wounds, explosions and sharp instruments.

Alimon encompasses the one to be protected in mercy and sheltering love. His wings appear almost as great impenetrable glass plates, sculpted like the facets of a diamond. They surround the recipient of his blessing like an extensive crystal dome. Hurtful missiles simply glance off these geometrically aligned walls.

Reivtip is like a powerful centre of angelic gravity who protects the complete integrity of those who seek her blessing.

Tafthi turns away things that cause hurt by stabbing and penetration. His shining hands strike decisively at them as they lunge and threaten, and turn them off course.

The Celtic Deities

⊕ Bran
⊕ Brigid

Bran lost his life in an earthly conflict, yet he embraced resurrection and became an eternal protector and guardian of his people. For this blessing, the magical qualities of the head of Bran are emphasized. His unwavering focus and monumental protection descend upon the invocator. He is in every sense Bran the Blessed, Bran of Blessings (see page 61).

Brigid, whose name we call on for each of the blessing scrolls, is particularly honoured as Woman of Compassion and Woman of Fiery Protection for this blessing. Goddess of light and wisdom, she will cast her radiant aura around the person who is to be safeguarded.

Decoration Ideas

Whether you want to decorate a shortened scroll for display purposes or a full-length scroll for secretion, here are some ideas to inspire you.

The scarab (a beetle depicted within a ring symbolizing the circle of the sun) is an ancient device for safeguarding soldiers, as is the image of a bear, which is a sigil for strength and watchfulness. The bloodstone is the most famous of all talismans for those undertaking military endeavours, and a tiny tumbled bloodstone attached to this blessing scroll would be highly appropriate. The sacred Monogramme of Thoth, God of Wisdom and Enlightenment, is in the shape of a Tau cross (a 'T') standing on a circle. It was known as a very powerful sigil, particularly guarding against hidden dangers and the occurrence of ambush, since it symbolized the God of Wisdom and Foresight presiding over the world and eternally protecting it.

For the angels, their protection is signified by these symbols:
- ⊕ *Michael:* a shield
- ⊕ *Shekinah:* a circle of light containing an equal-sided cross of light
- ⊕ *Zazriel:* a shining face
- ⊕ *Ribkiel:* the wheel of the sun
- ⊕ *Alimon:* a diamond
- ⊕ *Rievtip:* a dot within a circle
- ⊕ *Tafthi:* praying hands surrounded by a halo

For the Celtic deities, their signs are:

⊕ *Brigid:* an equal-sided cross of light within a ring of light

⊕ *Bran:* a golden pyramid

A suitable crystal would be a bloodstone, which connects to the angelic spheres of shielding, stability, healing and sanctuary.

Appropriate aromatic oils would be rosemary, which connects to the angelic spheres of protection and clarity, and lavender, which is connected to the angelic spheres of protection, consolation and wellbeing.

Writing the Blessing

Before starting work on your blessing scroll, you will have assembled and blessed your materials, prayed to Brigid and Michael and intoned the Supplication to the Celtic Deities. Now intone the Rune of Intent:

'As I, (say your name), inscribe this scroll, I affirm that my act is holy, my heart pure, and my words vessels which I pray will be filled and blessed with the power of valiant Michael, Brightness of the Mountains, and Brigid of the Mantle, she who dwells in the golden heart of the sun. May Brigid and Michael bless and protect me and the work that I seek to achieve.'

Then write the Blessing:

'Valiant Michael of the white steeds
Shekinah of loveliest grace,
Zazriel of the strength of the Presence,
Ribkiel of the Will of God,
Alimon of the shielding might,
Rievtip of the glorious steadfastness,

Tafthi of the Sacred Hands:
Bless, thou chiefs of generous chiefs,
Myself and everything around me,
Bless me in all my actions,
In every enterprise,
Throughout every campaign,
In all my comings and goings,
Vehicle-bourne or walking,
Waiting or watching,
Active or passive,
Waking and sleeping.
Make Thou me safe for ever,
Make Thou me safe for ever.

Ring of angels of the mightiest valour,
All those whom I have named,
Oh! Save me until the end of my day.
Oh! Save me until the end of my day.'

(Note that in addition to the Blessing, you will also write the Supplication to the Celtic Deities and a one-line prayer to Brigid and Michael, both below in italic type.)

Intone the Prayer to Brigid and Michael:

'In the name of Brigid the Shining One,
In the name of the Great Chief,
I ask that my prayer for blessing be heard.
I ask that you purify my intention
And make my mind a mountain pool of clarity,
The fish in it leaping and silver
To summon the brightness of the blessing

From the hills of the angels.
May the Archangel Michael, and Brigid the Radiant
In whom dwells the presence of Divine Mother,
Of their benevolence,
Hear and grant my prayer.
By Brigid, by the Great Chief of the Angels, may it be so.'

Write the Supplication to the Celtic Deities:

'Bran, four-square strong,
Mighty peak of spiritual attainment,
Stand between this (insert rank and name)
And all encroaching harm.

Brigid of Blessings
Abide with (as above).
Woman of Compassion,
Woman of all-encircling Grace,
Surround (as above) with thy radiant fire
Of protective Love.'

Finish the scroll by writing the words:

'By Brigid and by Michael, Great Chief of the Angels, may it be so.'

Now you can decorate the scroll as you wish, before secreting
the full-length scroll and displaying a shortened version of the
scroll (if made) using the wording on p.196. Note, however, that
the full blessing is of a suitable length to be accommodated by
the display scroll.

SHORTENED BLESSING FOR THE DISPLAY SCROLL

'Valiant Michael of the white steeds
Shekinah of loveliest grace,
Zazriel of the strength of the Presence,
Ribkiel of the Will of God,
Alimon of the shielding might,
Rievtip of the glorious steadfastness,
Tafthi of the Sacred Hands:

Bless, thou chiefs of generous chiefs,
Myself and everything around me,
Bless me in all my actions,
In every enterprise,
Throughout every campaign,
In all my comings and goings,
Vehicle-bourne or walking,
Waiting or watching,
Active or passive,
Waking and sleeping.
Make Thou me safe for ever,
Make Thou me safe for ever.

Ring of angels of the mightiest valour,
All those whom I have named,
Oh! Save me until the end of my day.
Oh! Save me until the end of my day.'

A COMPENDIUM
OF ANGELS

Afriel
Attributes: an angel of the supreme power of the heavens; the children's angel
Symbols: pearls, wheat ears, white rose petals, a ring of angels

Alimon
Attributes: Alimon encompasses people in mercy and love.
Symbols: a diamond

Ambriel
Attributes: an enfolding, bridging angel who manifests the twinned mirror aspects of our deeper soul reality
Symbols: a silver arched bridge surmounted by a golden spiral

Anael
Attributes: angel of the mystery at the heart of the rose; the angel of the star of love
Symbols: a full-blown red rose with golden sepals

Anahita
Attributes: the angel of fruitfulness
Symbols: an apple tree in its late-summer fruitfulness

Ananchel
Attributes: exudes a healing silence and wears many radiant crowns from which flow a multitude of blessings; angel of grace
Symbols: a bright crown encircled with a ring of white doves

Anauel
Attributes: presides over commercial success and prosperity
Symbols: a shower of golden light

Anthriel
Attributes: a beautiful angel of harmony and balance
Symbols: a depiction of the number 8 in silver-violet

Ardousius
Attributes: the divine feminine spirit who presides over childbirth
Symbols: jewels, a star emanating rays

Armisael
Attributes: the angel of the womb; head of the birthing angels
Symbols: the full moon

Azara
Attributes: helps to balanced the right and left sides of the brain
Symbols: a tree with invisible roots penetrating into the earth

Baglis
Attributes: the angel of temperance; restores emotional balance
Symbols: a still lake reflecting serene blue skies

Balthial
Attributes: surrounds us with the healing balm of forgiveness
Symbols: an extending hand offering a bright jewel

Barakiel
Attributes: laugher, good humour, benevolence
Symbols: a smiling winged face

Barbelo
Attributes: the angel of abundance
Symbols: a celestial spring with a flow of gold down to Earth

Brigid
Attributes: glorious golden being, both angel and goddess
Symbols: wheat ears, pearls, a lily, a rose, a dandelion, an oyster-catcher, rowan berries, a rowan tree, a Brigid's cross

Butator
Attributes: presides over clarity and precision
Symbols: a magnifying glass, the number 10

Camaysar
Attributes: angel of domestic harmony
Symbols: encircling arms

Cambiel
Attributes: eccentric; like to surprise and startle; encourages thinking 'outside the box'
Symbols: a hand pointing upwards

Cathonic
Attributes: connects and grounds us in our endeavours; the angel of manifesting energy
Symbols: a pillar, ebony

Chamuel
Attributes: Works with Balthial to nurture tolerance and love
Symbols: flowering meadows, an ascending lark

Colopatiron
Attributes: angel of freedom, who unlocks prison doors
Symbols: a heart containing an open door

Cosmiel
Attributes: a magnificent angel who circumnavigates the cosmos
Symbols: enfolding wings, a star with a boat crossing its face

Derdekea
Attributes: a heavenly female power who descends to Earth for
the salvation of humanity; the Holy Grail – the Woman who is All
Symbols: a teardrop reflecting a star

Ecanus
Attributes: the angelic scribe
Symbols: an upright pen portrayed as a maypole with rainbow-
coloured streamers

Gabriel
Attributes: brings the mystical moon and its power of fertility
Symbols: a chaplet of roses

Gavreel
Attributes: angel of reconciliation
Symbols: a golden triangle, golden scales

Gazardiel
Attributes: angel of new beginnings, renewal and enlightenment
Symbols: the rising sun

Harahel

Attributes: mistress of learning, the angel of elevated knowledge, mental refinement and acuity, guardian of libraries, universities, archives and schools
Symbols: a silver bird

Hariel

Attributes: gentle, brooding angel of domestic animals
Symbols: a golden tree

Haurvatat

Attributes: the great angel, the personification of salvation
Symbols: a rose emitting light

Iahel

Attributes: the angel of meditation and illumination
Symbols: scattered jewels

Itkal

Attributes: inapires co-operation and affection
Symbols: a circle of dancing children

Liwet

Attributes: angel of our own individual uniqueness
Symbols: a clear gemstone reflecting a rainbow

Malachi

Attributes: stands in state in the sphere of finalities; he rules the beginning and then end point in the creational scheme.
Symbols: the ouroboros (a golden snake swallowing its tail)

Metatron
Attributes: the heavenly scribe; the Prince of the Divine Presence
Symbols: a jewelled book, a golden pen streaming with light

Michael (Archangel)
Attributes: chief of the angelic realms; brightest warrior; also known as Sabbathiel
Symbols: a winged disc, a three-cornered shield of light bearing the image of a golden crowned serpent

Mihael
Attributes: angel of fidelity
Symbols: a ring, a pair of swans

Mihr
Attributes: angel of friendship
Symbols: a jewelled cave

Mikhar
Attributes: presiding angel over the heavenly baptismal waters
Symbols: a dove, a mountain spring

Nihangius
Attributes: angel of the home; both masculine and feminine
Symbols: a hearth fire surrounded by angels

Nuriel
Attributes: 'white peace'
Symbols: a crown of white feathers

Omniel
Attributes: angel of marriage
Symbols: a lovers' knot

Phanuel
Attributes: angel of hope and joy; shines like a bright golden star
Symbols: an angelic countenance, smiling and illuminated with golden light

Pyrhea
Attributes: the angel of the life-force, initiating energy, fiery inspiration
Symbols: a ruby, a tower of flame, drops of blood

Rachiel
Attributes: angel of sexual joy and devotion
Symbols: a flame

Raphael (Archangel)
Attributes: Lord of the Book of Truth, Giver of Laws and Master of the Word of Maa Kheru
Symbols: a miniature golden scroll, a caduceus

Rampel
Attributes: radiates wisdom, steadfastness, ancientness, strength and masterful stillness
Symbols: a mountain

Reivtip
Attributes: like a powerful centre of angelic gravity who protects the complete integrity of those who seek her blessing.
Symbols: a dot within a circle

Remiel
Attributes: angel of lost souls
Symbols: a net of stars

Ribkiel
Attributes: a mighty angel who drives the divine chariot
Symbols: a face emanating rays in the form of a wheel

Rochel
Attributes: darts like a silver fish in a stream
Symbols: a fish with golden eyes emitting sun rays

Sabriel
Attributes: chief of the order of Tarshishim, the 'brilliant ones'
associated with the virtues. Sabriel, shining with the light of a
thousand stars, overcomes and banishes, returning the soul to its
pristine state of ease, peace and grace
Symbols: fire-speaking tongues

Samandiriel
Attributes: angel of fertility of inspiration and the gifting of
inspiration one to one another
Symbols: an orb reflecting stars; an egg with the golden ring of
infinity secreted within it

Sandalphon (Archangel)
Attributes: great bright gentle yet mighty angel of the Earth and
angel of the embryo; has all guardian angels in her/his care
Symbols: a garland, an orb

Shekinah (Archangel)
Attributes: star-bright archangel of grace and rarefied fire; angel of liberation and independence
Symbols: an ascending golden bird, a phoenix, a circle of light containing an equal-sided cross of light

Tafthi
Attributes: turns away things that cause hurt by stabbing and penetration. His shining hands strike decisively at them as they lunge and threaten, and turn them off course
Symbols: praying hands surrounded by a halo

Tual
Attributes: presides over Taurus and helps us to realize our aims in the material world; gives the bullish strength, determination and capacity for hard work needed to initiate and sustain a business.
Symbols: a ring through flaring nostrils surrounded by a halo

Tubiel
Attributes: sweet-voiced and of a silvery, subtle appearance, will call lost birds home
Symbols: a small many-coloured bird

Tuthiel
Attributes: the Angel Over Lost Things; has a bright, hovering appearance, like the radiant shimmer of a supernatural humming bird fanning the ethers as she seeks to perform her services in an ecstasy of joy.
Symbols: feathers

Valohel
Attributes: the angle of peace
Symbols: an ascending dove, the starlit heavens

Zadkiel
Attributes: the angel of transformation associated with the Holy Grail; benevolence, mercy, laughter, healing, resurrection, divine nourishment
Symbols: a violet flame

Zazriel
Attributes: an angelic prince, mounted on horseback, representing the divine strength, might and power
Symbols: huge footprints, a shining face, a crown of glory, a caparisoned war horse